# Making
# Fine
# Furniture

**Designer – makers and their projects**

# Making Fine Furniture

## Designer – makers and their projects

## Tom Darby

GUILD OF MASTER CRAFTSMAN PUBLICATIONS LTD

First published 1992 by Guild of Master Craftsman Publications Ltd,
Castle Place, 166 High Street, Lewes, East Sussex BN7 1XU
Reprinted 1993, 1998

© Tom Darby 1992

ISBN 0 946819 30 0

Illustrations by David Stokan

All photographs not otherwise credited on captions are by Tom Darby

Designed by Teresa Dearlove

Phototypesetting by Reprographic Centre, 8 Bond Street, Brighton

Printed in Hong Kong by H&Y Printing Ltd

# Contents

# Dedication

I would like to dedicate this book to my wife Margaret, who said to a doubting Thomas when the book was proposed, *Why not?*

# Acknowledgements

I would like to thank all the woodworkers who contributed to this book. Their hospitality and friendliness at our first meeting made me feel that this book could be written. I have appreciated their patience in dealing with my frequent requests for more information and the trust they have placed in me to faithfully reproduce their views and work.

My special thanks go to Leon Sadubin for his constant encouragement and for introducing me to David Stokan, whose brilliant drawings are a central feature of this book, and whose professional advice has been invaluable.

Elizabeth Inman as editor has been a sympathetic supporter and counsellor who has provided information and advice promptly on the innumerable occasions I have asked.

For their assistance with research, and the organisation which could provide information and photographs without delay, I would like to thank Grace Cochrane of the Powerhouse Museum, Sydney; Jane Hyden of the National Gallery, Canberra, and Pamille Berg of Mitchell, Giurgola and Thorp, architects for the New Parliament House, Canberra. I would also like to thank Mark Strizic and Gryphon Books for the photographs of the cabinet by Schulim Krimper, and Ruth and Paul Mitchell for permitting the Michael Gill settle to be photographed in their home.

To my wife Margaret and family, thanks for your encouragement and support, and those endless hours of quiet time which made the writing possible.

# Foreword

Many readers will undoubtedly share Tom Darby's enthusiasm for fine timbers and his admiration for those who work with them professionally. And many also know the pleasure of 'having a go' at making something beautiful and yet functional that can be used, passed on to the family or given to friends.

This book provides an intimate insight into the lives and working processes of some of the many designer-makers in Australia who are making a living in the 1990s through making furniture — but furniture whose central concern is wood and the skills and understanding that are necessary to work it well. Following the example of earlier practitioners like Robert Prenzel and Schulim Krimper, these designer-makers are part of a revival in studio furniture-making that started in Australia in the mid-1970s, influenced in part by John Makepeace and others in the United Kingdom, and James Krenov, Wharton Esherick and Wendell Castle in the United States.

At the same time, Australia has a long history of 'making-do'. Settlers cut off from familiar supplies were remarkably innovative in their use of unfamiliar timbers and recycled objects such as kerosene tins, cotton reels and packing cases to make necessary items for a new environment. Through economic necessity, and also because of the satisfaction of achievement, 'making-do' developed into a 'do-it-yourself' tradition in the post-war years, and for some time journals like *Homemaker*, *Australian Home Beautiful* and *Australian House and Garden* provided regular features on making furniture from published designs.

This book combines a glimpse into the ideals and practices of a number of professional makers with an opportunity to work through a special design that they have offered. These designer-makers use well-known common timbers, unusual minor species and even 'found' timbers with traces of previous uses still clinging to them to make new forms and new meanings in furniture. And almost everyone reading this book will know someone who treasures the hours spent in a home workshop and will recognise the special commitment of these people to their work.

**Grace Cochrane**
Curator, Australian Decorative Arts and Design, post-1945
Powerhouse Museum, Sydney

# Introduction

In a world where modern communications have blurred the edge of national identity, most countries have maintained at least some distinctly different cultural values and traditions in woodcrafts. Australia, with its short history, its dynamic mix of ethnic cultures, and the acceptance of individualism as a national characteristic, has fewer traditions than most to modify.

It is possible for a woodworker in Australia to be an individualist doing his or her own thing, and be readily accepted if the work has some intrinsic value. This creative freedom offers unique opportunities to an intuitive craftsman. No doubt such work has been influenced by the skill of others, if not by observing their work then through the great range of woodworking books and magazines now available. For any design or process to be unique, a craftsman would have had to have lived the life of a hermit, because we all build on the experiences of others, and most of the conscious decisions of designing and making made in the workshop are based on subconscious knowledge acquired beyond the creation of our own shavings and sawdust.

The twelve designer-makers who have contributed to this book have small successful workshops. They were interviewed in their workshops during November 1990, and the profiles drawn are of each as I found them, presented in part as a narrative of that day. I have given each a setting, as I found the workshop and home reflected the personality and creativity of its owner. Some have had little formal training, but all are recognised nationally for their contribution to wood design and excellence in craftsmanship. To have learned a craft through the self-realisation that 'to make, you must know', means that you have few preconceptions about what is possible or desirable. In turn this generates free thought and self-analysis. For the self-taught there are often few traditions to follow, for they are unknown, with few limitations on what constitutes the accepted skills of a craft.

The work displayed here is characteristic of Australian designer-makers and has been chosen for this reason, and I hope that what makes it distinctive will be appreciated as you read of the work and thoughts of these craftsmen. The designs they have created for this book have been worked in Australian cabinet timbers, and where appropriate I have suggested alternative timbers or have described characteristics which should make the selection of an alternative timber possible. Australian cabinet timbers are so stunning that going to the trouble of locating a supplier could add to the quality of your experience in making these pieces.

The designs selected are of functional furniture, some simple in construction and detail, others more complex for those who seek a challenge. Some of the designers have suggested a range of sizes and alternative construction details which would make the piece suitable for use in different situations. Although most of their workshops are equipped with an extensive range of machinery, the projects devised for this book can be worked in a modest workshop with relatively unsophisticated machine and hand tools.

The reader will require a modicum of workshop skills to construct each piece. There are many excellent reference books available which provide instruction in those skills, and as a consequence in this book only special techniques considered peculiar to the construction of each project are described in detail.

**Refectory table, Leon Sadubin.**
Photographer: Scott Donkin.

The sculptured detail on an edge of timber was all I saw. Shading the glass with my hand, I realised it was the top of a long table. Whether it was that tantalising glimpse or the whirring of the air conditioner above my head which induced me to enter the shop, I cannot remember. The air inside was a chilling contrast to the steamy heat of a Sydney summer day. I felt sorry for the proprietress as the table which filled the window was covered with vine baskets, and when these had been removed there was little space for us to stand. I thanked her and she retreated to her desk.

As I eased the table away from the window I marvelled at how light it felt, as it looked three metres long. I could not step away to see both base and top together, but among the clutter it was unlike any table I had seen before. The top was made from two consecutive flitches cut from a Tasmanian blackwood log, with the impression of a branch long dead visible in the shape and grain swirl of each piece. Both long edges had been lightly sculpted to emphasise grain movement without interfering with its pattern. Each defect was also shaped to flow in sympathy with the rest, yet my eye was not drawn to these details, so subtle was the treatment. The whole top was made to be touched, and on reflection it was a truly sensual experience. I had not previously seen such a soft lustrous finish, with a slight sheen but no reflections! You could look down into the surface, move your head, and refracted light brought to life the browns, greys and reds deep in the timber.

Kneeling was not easy in those confines, but the shape of the table legs, like the top, was determined by the tree, neatly balanced and organic. The whole table was *of* the tree, not timber shaped to a geometric form. With great difficulty I found the maker's card secured to the underside — 'Leon Sadubin, Thornleigh, New South Wales 1977'.

Thanking the proprietress, I left feeling that I had seen something unique on a day which previously had held no more promise than a damp shirt. Little did I know that that chance visit would, in the future, direct my attitudes, understanding and experiences in so many ways. That day, in a design sense I crossed the Rubicon.

On reflection, I realise that before that experience in 1977, my idea of furniture was defined by the English and Scandinavian styles I had admired so often in *Mobilia* and other design magazines. My upbringing had been conservative Anglo–Celtic, with heavy simple furniture in our home. The design courses I had studied in my youth had been retrospective: to learn by looking at what the lecturers promoted as the work of masters. While I recognise the value of this, there were few creative experiences offered, nor was I asked to discuss exhibits subjectively. This inadequate experience was 'design education' in 1950s Australia, and most Australians of my age share the same deprivation. It was not until fifteen years later, when I began to teach design to high school students, that a reassessment of what constituted the design process gave me different insights.

More recently I have tried to understand the influences directing the designs of contemporary woodworkers by reviewing the work of master craftsmen. Of Australian furniture made in the last century, there are few pieces which are not either Georgian–English reproductions or copies of that style. One outstanding exception to this is 'bush' furniture, typified by the 'Jimmy Possum' chair. With spindles made in a crude manner and the seat split from a flitch, it was a chair fundamental in the extreme, yet in its elegant simplicity it is not unlike the more elemental products of High Wycombe, or the Shaker settlements of New England, or the Irish comb-back chairs. Michael Gill describes this chair as being 'more air than chair', and its authentic simplicity is in stark contrast to other attempts made at that time to adapt designs from the 'Old Country' using Australian timbers.

Little wonder the early settlers and cabinetmakers in Australia found the native timbers difficult to work. There are many references in 19th-century journals to the great durability and strength of blue gum, box, mahogany and she-oak, but an equal number of qualifying statements about their weight, difficult grain, unusual seasoning characteristics, dimensional instability and checking. With the discovery of the more easily worked cedar and Huon pine, which had similar properties to exotic timbers such as mahogany and satinwood, came finer furniture, but fashion dictated the use of imported known timbers for most prestigious commissions. This was partly because of prejudice against colonial timbers, and partly because the working properties of exotic timbers were more familiar to cabinetmakers who had served their apprenticeship in Great Britain. Little was known of native timbers and few timber dealers could identify species accurately in the forest, relying rather on classification of sawn boards as suitable for specific uses. (Most countries which were established as

colonies of a European nation were subject to the same cultural transfer of skills, knowledge and culture.)

The all-pervading British influence in Australia persisted until long after the granting of statutory independence in 1901. A true sense of independent national identity did not appear until after World War II, and very few Australians prior to 1950 questioned the immutable link which existed with Great Britain. Should we be surprised, therefore, that until the dislocation caused by World War II our British heritage affected our attitudes to life, even down to determining our choice of domestic furniture? That dislocation precipitated an influx of non-English-speaking immigrants, changing forever the structure of Australian society. Nationalist feelings grew and a new national identity evolved, the product of a dynamic mix of peoples and a realisation that geographically we are part of the Asia–Pacific region. Since 1970 there has been much public debate and personal enquiry as to what it is to be an Australian, with an increased interest in all things Australian. The furniture designs displayed in this book are an expression of this new identity.

**Fireplace surround, Queensland black bean, Robert Prentzel, 1910, Australian National Gallery, Canberra.**

Who were the first to incorporate in their furniture design elements which were peculiarly Australian? Two outstanding Melbourne cabinetmakers initiated a change in public perception of contemporary furniture before 1960. Their work was commissioned by an appreciative and influential clientele, giving them the public status of artist-craftsmen, yet both broke with tradition by incorporating intrinsically Australian features in their furniture. Strangely, both were German, although their individual contributions were very different.

Robert Prenzel trained as a cabinetmaker in Prussia and came to Melbourne in 1888. Between 1910 and 1930 he designed many pieces of furniture in the Art Nouveau style. Although some craftsmen had previously used native flora and fauna as decorative motifs, he was the first to develop these into an acknowledged art form. He experimented with a wide range of native timbers, and his sympathetic use of jarrah, rosewood, silky oak and mountain ash added a distinctive quality to his furniture.

Schulim Krimper, an Austrian-trained master craftsman, migrated to Australia in 1939 and was soon producing distinctive one-off pieces of contemporary domestic furniture. His experience in Berlin of the modern style of northern Europe was evident in the elegant simplicity of his designs. The

**Detail of cabinet, Schulim Krimper. Finger grips are carved into the outer edges of the drawer fronts.**
Photographer: Mark Strizic.

acquisition of a chest and sideboard by the National Gallery of Victoria in 1948 was the first contemporary furniture acquired by a museum in Australia. Although some imported timbers were used, he demonstrated for the first time the potential of native timbers, as their colour, grain and figure became an integral part of the total design. For Krimper, the design details in a piece were suggested by the character of the wood itself. He was known to wax lyrical to clients about the beauty in a piece of timber to be used in a commission, and had a sculptor's

**Cabinet, black bean, Schulim Krimper, wax finished.**
Photographer: Mark Strizic.

sympathy for his medium. He often altered designs during construction when a knot or grain swirl, revealed during timber preparation, prompted a different interpretation. Every piece was meticulously finished by hand sanding and waxing to leave a soft surface. This treatment was ideal for the hard, dense native timbers he used. The recognition given to Krimper in the 1950s and 1960s heightened public awareness of designer-made furniture and set a standard to which others could aspire.

Although individualism in Australia had been a national characteristic since the last century, it was mostly expressed in overt behaviour and was not particularly obvious in our homes, where we tended to be peculiarly conformist. It was not until the 1950s that, like other countries, Australia was influenced by Scandinavian design. This coincided in the late 1960s with an increase in disposable income for a proportion of the population, in turn providing the patronage which enabled a small number of individual designer-makers to establish workshops. Also, the conformity of the furniture industry created a void which was filled by the new designer-makers, who principally worked in solid timbers on small commissions negotiated with individual clients. Unlike Krimper, most worked alone, but they shared his passion for wood, many moving themselves physically out of the city to be closer to forest and timber mill.

Some were initially attracted to the craft by its popular image as an alternative lifestyle. These fantasies of an idyllic existence no doubt induced many disaffected professionals but sustained few, as they soon realised that there was more to producing saleable furniture than good intentions and a warm feeling. Others made conscious decisions to alter their career path in search of a more satisfying profession, and brought skills of design, scholarship, marketing and promotion to their new careers.

Whatever the reason for making a change, those few who survived the initial financial strictures and frustrations as designer-makers found patronage from appreciative clients and led the new movement in Australian furniture design. It is surprising how few followed the path of 'apprentice cabinetmaker to master craftsmen'. Perhaps this says something significant about the limitations of trade training in this country and the professional attitude it has often failed to engender.

Who are these designer-makers, and is their work really unique? If so, why? The Australian landscape is often characterised for overseas visitors as having an intense white light, deep shade and bush which is gnarled. This is far from the truth, as the great contrast in climates and topography ensures an infinite variety of landscape. The character of each craftsman is directly related to his environment, whether it be the soft light and Gothic landscape of Tasmania, the warm humid glades of the coast of New South Wales, or the sandy beaches and hinterland of Western Australia. Perhaps this is why I find such diversity in the work of craftspeople in this country.

Anyone who works professionally and sympathetically with wood must have some feeling for the environment which produced it. Walk through the Australian bush or forest with many of these designer-makers, and you are likely to experience a new awakening to its sounds, smells and tactile nature. These people have a peculiar awareness of its sensuality and express this with an intensity which would have been quite foreign 30 years ago. At that time you may have heard a potter talking of his medium 'relating to mother earth', but very few woodworkers related in a similar manner to the forest which produced their medium. Perhaps this is a natural extension of Krimper's beliefs, using modern idiom and a related awareness initiated by the conservation movement. But no matter what its origin, this new feeling for nature has had a dynamic impact on the work of most modern designer-makers.

This heightened awareness is not experienced with the same intensity by all, or with the same effect. To understand the reasons for this, let us return to Leon Sadubin's table made in 1977. For me, that piece initiated a quest for other examples of furniture which would excite me in the same way. Strangely, I did not find them. Certainly pieces I had seen at exhibitions and displays were well made, and most were clever, but very few satisfied the purpose of that quest. This left me feeling rather awkward at exhibitions. Most fellow viewers were fulsome in their praises, while I had this odd feeling that I had seen it all before somewhere. By this I do not mean that the work of those exhibiting was not original or that they were re-exhibiting pieces many times over. Rather, in most there seemed to be a common influence, an 'exotic likeness' which made you turn from one piece to another and not sense a transition of expression. I believe I now understand what that likeness is, but it left me bemused for years.

When a piece of furniture impresses me at an exhibition, I often ask myself, why? How you feel about a piece of furniture or music, or a work of art, is idiosyncratic. Either something moves you or it leaves you unaffected. Often explaining your likes and dislikes involves exposing your feelings or emotions. The expression, 'I like what I like' is a valid comment about all that we experience *only* if that assessment is based on a broad pattern of experiences which is not limiting. I view things with the eyes of an Australian, eyes which I inherited from my English-born parents, but my understandings and sensibilities are the product of the total pattern of experiences acquired throughout life. My response to furniture is an intuitive appreciation based on those experiences, and as a consequence my interpretation is different to that of a person from another culture, and often from other Australians. This does not mean that I do not appreciate the beauty of things un-Australian, but I am peculiarly affected by things which I sense are 'quintessentially Australian'. I hope after reading *all* of this book that, through the exposition of these Australian woodworkers, you can share this 'feeling for things Australian'.

The very name Dundurrabin sounds romantic, to Australians at least, as it has that Aboriginal rhythm suggestive of the outback and space. In reality it is a small village set on the western rim of the Dorrigo Plateau at a point where it intrudes into the mountain wilderness. To the north and west are unpopulated and forested mountain ranges which stretch to the Queensland border, an area the size of Switzerland. Dundurrabin is an ideal place for Robert Parker, forester, conservationist and furniture-maker, to live.

Romantic it may sound, but a day working with him is sufficient to make you reconsider your romanticism. We had set off from Robert's home in the four-wheel-drive utility truck for a 30-kilometre ride over jarring roads into the Cloud's Creek State Forest. The lunchbox and chainsaw clattered noisily on the tray behind and the wheels threw up showers of stones as we turned off the road on to a forest track. Most of the giant trees were gone, but occasionally an ancient tallowwood, its top torn off and its trunk hollowed, overhung the track. A regrowth hoop pine stood out amongst the eucalypts as the forest crowded in on either side.

We pulled up on a straight section of road as another vehicle blocked our way. The district forestry officer was standing waiting for us. He had come to give Robert approval for the felling of a long-dead rosewood tree which unfortunately stood near the boundary of a nature reserve within the forest. The problem was to accurately locate that boundary, established by a cartographer in an office many years before and perhaps never surveyed. We knew only that it was to the east of the road we were standing on. Robert found the rosewood tree without trouble, then we set off in search of 'blazed' trees which might mark the reserve boundary. The forester was a helpful, friendly fellow, who was obviously familiar with this type of ramble as he scampered over giant fallen logs, long rotten and dangerous. 'Watch out, that's a stinger,' but the advice was too late as the bush brushed my arm but thankfully missed my face. For the remainder of the day I had a red weal on my wrist and forearm which burnt painfully. We eventually retreated to the road to consult maps once more, and to roll down socks and pull up trouser legs to remove leeches. It was not very wet, so I had only one inside my sock, but Robert removed a large tick from his back and me one from my head. Then back looking for those blazes once more. This time I chose a pathway laced with a blackjack vine. Its barbed tendrils clung to my boot and I took another step, leaving the boot entangled. As I unravelled the vine from my boot, Robert told the story of not preparing a fully-cleared escape route before felling a tree. When the tree started to fall, in his haste to clear the danger zone he ran into a blackjack vine which removed his shirt and a considerable amount of skin as he fought to get away. I looked up from replacing my boot, and my heart skipped a beat. No one was there! I began looking for tracks and finally heard faint voices down a gully.

We never did find that boundary, but we did locate a beefwood tree recently felled in a storm, which Robert wanted approval to mill. Once more we retreated to the road, de-leeched ourselves and headed back to Dundurrabin. My shin was sore, the result of a fall into a rotten log, the stinger burn was looking angry and my sock was full of blood from leeches. The romantic notions of a serene life as forester evaporated as the sweat dried on my shirt. We had not done any work, lifted that great chainsaw or carried those heavy flitches of timber from the forest, just walked around in circles. Robert's strong shoulders and forearms give me reason to doubt my own ability to endure a day working there. The most unsettling sensation of that morning was when I had replaced my boot and looked up to find no one in sight. It gave me an instant sinking feeling, not knowing which way the road was, heavy cloud overhead and no sun to guide me. In that instant I recreated in my mind the great Australian legend of 'lost in the bush', in which I was the central character.

Robert and his wife Maree came to Dundurrabin as counsellors for a 'personal growth' group, some of the many in search of an alternative lifestyle in the 1970s. Robert was disaffected with surveying as a career, and Maree was a designer of woollen knitwear. As was often the case, the idyllic climate of the north coast of New South Wales, good intentions and warm feelings were not enough to maintain the original enthusiasm, and the group disbanded. Robert and Maree were loath to return to the city, and the new skills they had learned gave them the key to a more permanent place in the bush. They had roofed their own dwelling with shingles split in the forest and Robert began cutting shingles commercially. By degrees he found he liked working in the bush and exploring the forests. He bought a chainsaw mill and began milling and seasoning timber for the community and friends, finally making sculptured furniture with the few simple tools he had.

His family now live in a house which reflects his attachment to the forests and in which the detailing appears to have formed naturally from the timber. Walls are of posts and rails built from the adzed members of an old road bridge, infilled with hand-made mud bricks. The floor levels are joined with steps made from massive tallowwood flitches while a staircase climbs to a ceiling loft above, the spine made from a curved log with treads set into regular cuts up its length. A handrail made from a slender brush cypress sapling mimics the spine. Door and window catches are from hardwood off-cuts, each a different design, strong, functional and beautifully crafted. The furniture is of the same natural timber forms and looks as if it belongs there. Delicately he has transferred the forest to his home.

**Coffee table, blue gum.**
Photographer: Peter Derrett.

**Chair, hoop pine.**
Photographer: Peter
Derrett.

**Stool, Australian red
cedar and blackwood.**
Photographer: Peter
Derrett.

It is often said that necessity is the mother of invention. In the case of the Parkers' home that necessity was to build with what was readily available for little money. Robert's inventiveness or genius has been to design sympathetically with those found materials without compromise to design excellence. The lessons learnt in that home were translated with equal genius to his furniture.

Walking with Robert along a forest track or searching for boundaries in a forest reserve are enlightening experiences. He has an understanding of the forest which is reassuring in these times of conflict and confrontation over logging in native forests. The arguments on conservation of rainforests and sustainable forest management are polarising and confusing. Most conservationists want furniture made from beautiful timbers, but do not want these timbers taken from native forests. They are earnest in their arguments and motivated by worthy long-term aims, but many have a vision of forestry practice founded on passion rather than knowledge. Who can help but feel distressed as they watch a mature tree fall to a chainsaw or be affected by a hillside, once forested, now scattered with stumps and scarred earth? Fortunately for the conservation movement, most people react with the same feeling of revulsion. These simple and effective images are regularly presented to urban voters, through 60-second TV news clips which depict devastation in the forests. Anyone who cuts trees in a forest is branded as a villain in this simplistic presentation of an extremely complex problem.

The counterargument is put by the wood chippers and loggers, politically powerful and with sufficient backing to fund media campaigns and lobbying. Their message is that the forest is a valuable resource. To be fair, some have policies of managed forests as a renewable resource. Others, however, see it only as a raw material which will return profits on their vast capital investment, applying the same commercial principals as miners of iron ore. This approach ignores the presence of timbers of different qualities and uses, and treats the logs as a bulk amorphous resource having a profit determined only by cubic capacity. In Australia, as in most countries, the diverse position of the protagonists in this argument has steadily firmed or even retreated to more rigid policies and jaundiced propaganda. In the centre of this debate stands a small group with limited access to the media. One of this group is Robert Parker.

Both sides see Robert as a threat to their established position. His voice is small and his arguments are possibly too rational to gain acceptance, as both conservationists and the loggers see his proposals as the thin edge of the wedge. He is even derided by some of his conservationist friends for harvesting mature or dead trees, though they still use the timber he cuts and appreciate its beauty. He differs from many of the protagonists in his love of timber and trees, spending much of his time in the forest observing and learning.

Robert and I were standing on a ridge with a view across a valley to a distant ridge. 'That next ridge,' he said, 'was logged perhaps 40 years ago. The dominant species in the regrowth was Sydney blue gum, and in time the understorey of mixed rainforest species followed, firstly in protected gullies and later on the open ridge face. You can identify the rainforest canopy. It looks like a damp green cumulus cloud. Notice how the gums look unhealthy. Many individual trees have begun to "die back". The gums are stressed by competition from the dense undergrowth, but this is a natural process of evolution in a rainforest. If left undisturbed, the gums will continue to lose leaves, die and eventually fall. These trees can be harvested in a managed forest, which means less damage to the understorey if they're left to fall naturally. This can promote regrowth if the gums are taken as mature trees when the rainforest species are sufficiently mature to provide a replacement canopy.'

Most timber millers are primarily interested in through-put of timber in their mill and pay scant respect to the quality of the end product. As for the logger, he is given his orders, the tree is marked, and he uses a very expensive caterpillar tractor, operating at an inordinate hourly rate, to extract the fallen tree from the forest. This means the destruction of many sound rainforest trees which are in the path of the tractor. Robert's method of milling timber in the forest is too labour-intensive for anyone but small operators. Many in the conservation movement do not differentiate between Robert and the large commercial operators, and most want the native forests closed up in wilderness areas or national parks. Having a sensible discussion on this subject is difficult, even amongst friends.

As the principal of Cockatoo Creek Timbers, Robert has a vital interest in having continued access to forests, so he can sympathise with workers in the timber industry who are trying to protect their livelihood, and the Forestry Commission officers who are in an unenviable position of trying to satisfy politicians and pressure groups. He also believes that other aspects of forest management, like active reafforestation of rainforest species, have still to be seriously addressed by the industry. Robert collects seedlings of selected species in the forest, pots them in a hothouse adjacent to his home and replants them as advanced specimens to replace trees he logs.

To watch Robert work timber is a humbling and at times frightening experience. His skill with a chainsaw is prodigious. That most lethal of machines does precisely what he asks of it, whether it be trimming a burl in the forest or shaping a table

**Coffee table, tallowwood.**
Photographer: Lyn
Goodhope.

from a solid log. He shapes timber by 'wanding' the chainsaw across the surface, his touch so delicate with the one metre-long bar that the surface is only in need of sanding to finish. He is fully aware of the danger, but considers the chainsaw the most appropriate tool for shaping timber. His workshop is fundamental in the extreme, an open shed exposed to the elements, which in winter can include light snowfalls. An enormous bench, a simple woodturning lathe and bandsaw, some portable tools including a large belt sander and enormous power planer, and of course the ubiquitous chainsaw, are all that he uses.

He has little need for other tools, as most of his designs are organic forms replicating the shapes of timber in their natural state. For this the eye is more useful than a try-square and straightedge, but the trueness of his chairs bears witness to an uncanny ability at assessing angles and profiles. His work does not have to be true in a conventional sense, but correct in proportion and line.

Robert rarely sketches, drawing occasionally on the back of abrasive paper ideas he wants recorded. The concepts are formed in his mind and suggested by the timber, relying on the backsides and backs of others to prove the worth of his design. 'I design from the material,' he says, 'and I don't follow fashion. To do this is to invite the design to become inorganic. What's the use of making furniture from wood if the piece is in a shape which could have been made from plastic or steel? Probably it would have been better to make it from an alternative material and leave the timber in the forest.'

Simplicity is the keynote in his designs, using the least number of elements possible. He enjoys the challenge provided by chairs, and asks you to judge the success of his distinctive blade-backed chairs by sitting in one. They are not only comfortable but robust and stable. As all his chairs are made without leg rails, the seat is the critical structural member. He selects this piece carefully to ensure it is dense-fibred and defect-free. It is thicker than would normally be found in a chair, but the edges are heavily splayed and carefully profiled to give the seat a deceptively slender appearance. He is particularly proud of the chairs which have only two vertical blades as backs, as they eliminate the back rail used in a conventional chair. This back rail, he believes, is always a problem, as it is not possible to either shape or locate it at the correct height to be comfortable for everybody.

His tables, shaped with the chainsaw from solid logs so large that they must be turned with a bar, are often worked in the open. They are moved into the workshop when thoroughly dry and ready for final finishing. When finished they give little hint of their original gross size, and although still robust in section they are skilfully shaped to give the impression of a small domestic table rather than a shaped log. To see these tables in log form, with marker pen markings defining the final shape, and then to view the beautifully finished end product, gives you a better appreciation of Robert's considerable skill in designing by eye.

Robert is an ardent surfer, and escapes to the coast most weekends. He admits, 'There's something exquisite about sitting on your surfboard watching the swell and waiting for a wave and riding it when it comes. It's another form of self-expression. Relating to nature in a different way to being at home, but it's somehow similar to the feeling you get when you create something in the workshop that you know is just right.'

He is as animated when talking about surfing as he is about furniture or forests. The arguments he puts about the latter are forcefully presented and are based on strongly-held convictions — convictions which come from an understanding of nature which few can match but many are willing to challenge. His love of the forest and timber comes through faithfully with each statement, whether expressed in words, his furniture or his home.

It is a pity that his beliefs and understanding are not more widely circulated among pressure groups and those deciding the fate of forests in Australia. Perhaps all woodworkers worldwide, as responsible users of the products of native forests, should develop an informed opinion on this subject and express it forcefully.

**Carved bowl, rosewood.**
Photographer: Lyn Goodhope.

**Chair, blackwood.**
Photographer: Lyn Goodhope.

# Desk

**Rosewood desk,
© Robert Parker.**
Photographer: Lyn
Goodhope.

ost woodworkers choose the timber for a project after deciding what it is they want to make. Robert Parker is in the enviable position of having a forest at his disposal, so it is natural that he should begin with an idea *and* a tree, either standing or on the forest floor. In this case Robert was to make a desk, but its shape and form were suggested by the butt of the tree itself. Most of the trees he harvests are old or have died and many are

therefore hollow with thin walls at the butt. Man has copied this natural form when designing strong, thin-walled structures like the cooling towers at thermal power stations, which are broad at the base and narrow slowly as the structure rises. Robert admits, 'I have long loved the shape of cooling towers. They make great pedestals, if a trifle big. For some perverse reason, I think they were the inspiration for the pedestals in my desk.'

If you have any intention of making a

desk identical or even similar to Robert's, be warned: you will require not only a suitable tree but also lifting equipment, or some ingenuity. If you have access to a tree, it may be possible to remove most of the waste in the forest, which should make the removal of the pedestals to your workshop a

to define both the size and shape of your desk. To achieve a suitably-sized pedestal from a small log it may be possible to cooper the pedestal from sections of timber, but the difficulty of matching grain and making gap-free glued joints will add materially to the degree of difficulty in

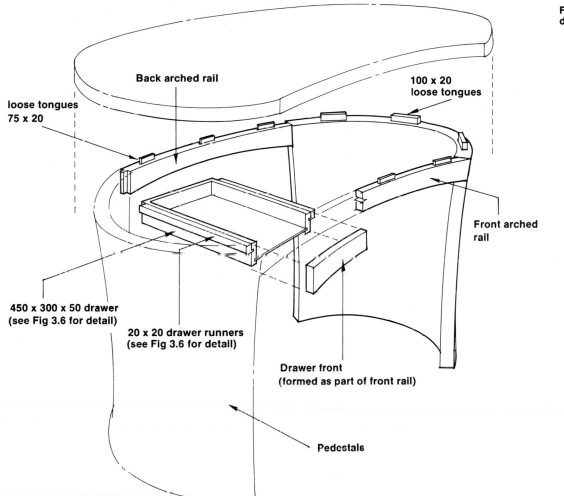

**Fig 3.1 Anatomy of the desk.**

Back arched rail

loose tongues
75 x 20

100 x 20
loose tongues

Front arched
rail

450 x 300 x 50 drawer
(see Fig 3.6 for detail)

20 x 20 drawer runners
(see Fig 3.6 for detail)

Drawer front
(formed as part of front rail)

Pedestals

heavy, but not impossible, task. Robert simplified the shaping by using a 3-tonne overhead crane, which may not be readily available in the workshops of most woodworkers. A log of this size can however be turned with a bar, and with careful planning the number of turns required to shape the pedestals can be reduced to a minimum. Heavy equipment may simplify the task, but it is not essential.

Although the drawings included here give dimensions and define the shape, you would be wise to use these only as a guide and to allow, as Robert Parker did, the tree

making the desk. If you wish to retain the size and shape of Robert's desk, it would be better to scale the desk to suit the log or search for a more suitable log. Robert Parker does most of his shaping with an electric chainsaw with a 400mm bar, using his eye to keep the curves consistent and the shape true. If you are not proficient at shaping by wanding with a chainsaw across a surface, you may need to practise on a waste log. By holding the chainsaw bar tangent to the surface and moving it from side to side across the surface, while keeping the bar moving with the teeth just in touch with the surface, complex curves can be cut. The hand controlling the saw is moved up and down, changing the angle of the bar to the horizontal while the bar is tangent to the curve. With care and practice a control can be achieved over the saw which will produce a continuous flowing curve with a *smooth* surface.

The rosewood used in this desk is straight-grained, which simplifies shaping, sanding and finishing. Robert has also used blue gum, cedar and tallowwood for tables of similar form without experiencing difficulties. Any timber with similar tangential and radial drying rates would be satisfactory, while timber with prominent medullary rays could be the most troublesome. While you may not have access to a forest, it may be possible to select a log at a timber mill and negotiate the acquisition of a butt of sufficient length to make the pedestals. Robert made the top of his desk from two book-matched flitches, but the top could be made from planks if they are carefully selected to match colour and grain. The effect will not be as *organically* desirable as Robert's solution, but if the colour is uniform the total effect will be satisfactory.

## Making the desk

There are only six components in the desk: the two pedestals, a top, front and back rails and a drawer. Tenons on the ends of the rails fit into mortices in the pedestals, while the top is jointed to the pedestals using loose tongues. Dowels or mortice and tenons would also be suitable methods of joining these components. The drawer is conventional in construction and is slung from the underside of the desk top.

### Making the pedestals

• Robert Parker used a log which was hollow and already in two segments. If your log is whole, it would be best cut into segments from which each pedestal can be made. The wall thickness of the segments should be not be less than 100mm, to allow for shaping.

• The pedestals are to finish at 715mm long, so a butt, or segments of a butt, should be cut to lengths of approximately 800mm.

• Mark the shape of the pedestal with a marker pen on the end of each segment, sighting the edges down the log to ensure that the curve on the top edge will be directly above the curve on the bottom edge. Remember that the size will be determined by the timber you are working with and the shape composed of free-form curves which are pleasing to the eye. If you wish to create the shape shown in these drawings, make templates for both pedestals (they are not mirror images) and continually check your progress in shaping. The *correctness* of the final shape should be judged by assessing whether the two pedestals complement each other when viewed standing in their final positions.

• Robert commenced shaping by cutting slabs from the outside with a chainsaw, tangential to the line marked on the end. Splitting wedges and an adze could be used. Cuts can be made close to the line and straight down the outside of the butt, as the final shaping will be carried out later.

• Mark the longitudinal curved shape with a marker pen on the edges, continuing the curve around the top and bottom edges as shown in Fig 3.2. The two lines should give a uniform thickness of 70mm.

• To shape the inside surface, cut longitudinal grooves down the inside face as shown in Fig 3.2, and remove the waste between the grooves with a splitting wedge. As the inside curve is longitudinally convex, cut each groove deeper at the ends than at the centre. The bottom of the grooves can be used as a depth gauge for final shaping. Final shaping is done with an adze and/or by wanding a chainsaw across the surface.

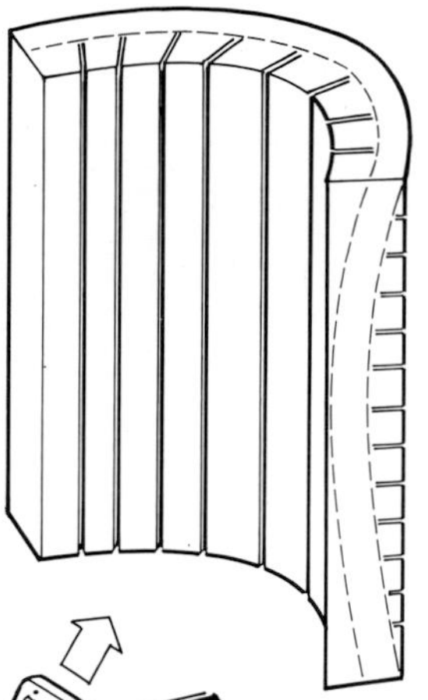

• To shape the outside surface, mark lines 50mm apart across the edge as shown in Fig 3.2. Set the depth of cut on a portable circular saw to the profile of the curve at a number of equally spaced intervals and make cuts around the outside of the shape parallel to an end. The profile produced by these saw kerfs will provide a guide when chainsawing or adzing the outside shape. Place the pedestal on its side and wand the surface to the shape shown in Fig 3.3 with a chainsaw.

• Check that the wall thickness is uniform or slightly thinner at the middle rather than the ends. This should minimise end splitting. Paint the end grain with Mobil Cer-M or some other industrial wax or acrylic paint, to slow end-grain drying. Stand the pedestals aside until thoroughly seasoned and dry.

• Round over the long edges of each pedestal with a plane, spokeshave or drawknife, and sand all curved surfaces with a drawknife and belt sander. Finish by hand sanding to a fine finish.

• To cut the pedestals to a final length, place each pedestal upright on a smooth surface, wedging the bottom edge if necessary to make the pedestal stand correctly. With a short 25mm thick batten on the floor adjacent to the side of the pedestal, mark a line parallel to the floor around both internal and external surfaces as shown in Fig 3.4. With the pedestal on its side, cut to the line with a saw and plane the end grain to a finished, flat surface.

• Stand the pedestal on the cut end, and using a scribing stock similar to that shown in Fig 3.4, mark a line around the top end. Cut this end and finish as before.

• Using a straight bit in a router, cut three 42mm deep uniformly spaced trenches in the top end of each pedestal for the 75mm x 20mm loose tongues

Fig 3.2 Saw cuts used to guide shaping of the pedestals.

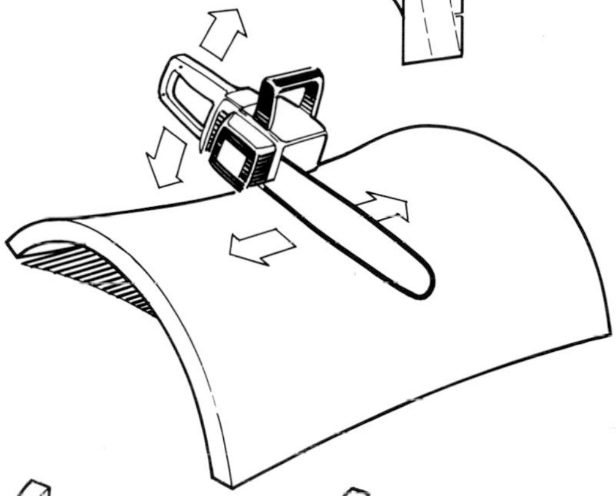

Fig 3.3 Wanding with a chainsaw to shape the pedestals.

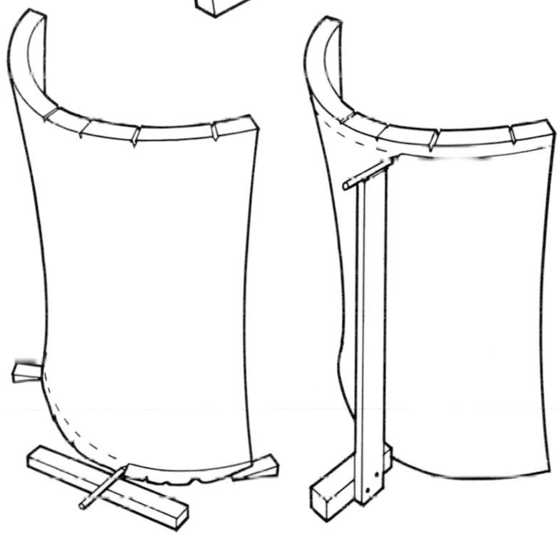

Fig 3.4 Marking the pedestals to length.

shown in Fig 3.5. Make the 70mm long loose tongues to fit these trenches.

## Making the top

• The top of the desk is made from two book-matched flitches of rosewood. As the finished width of the table is 950mm, each flitch is almost 500mm wide. If you are not able to find timber of this width, it will be necessary to edge-glue a number of boards, which should be carefully selected to match colour and grain — consecutive boards from the same flitch are ideal. As

Fig 3.5 Detailed
dimensions of the desk.

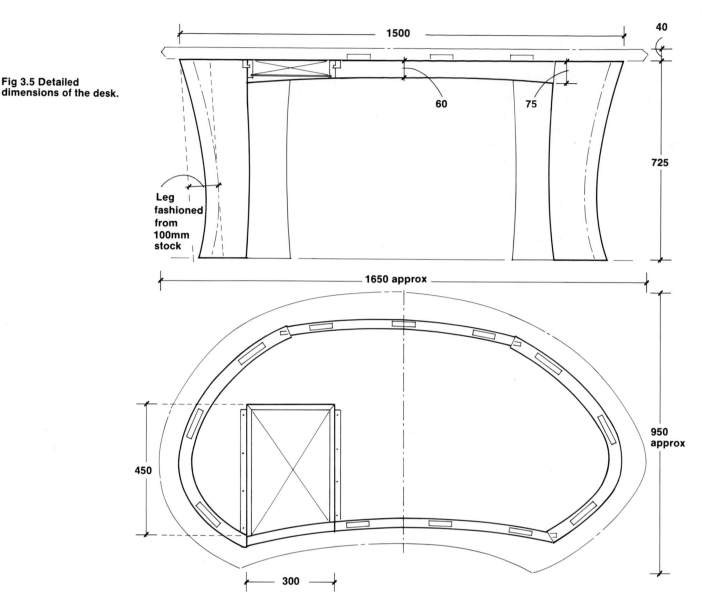

the desk top is to finish at 40mm
thick, the boards will need to be
approximately 50mm thick in their
sawn state.

● Dress one surface of each board
and dress an edge to form a gap-
free joint between adjacent boards.
Biscuits, dowels or a spline and
groove can be used to align and
strengthen the joint. If the desk top
is to be made from a number of
narrow boards, these can be
thicknessed to 40mm before
edge-gluing.

● Glue the joint (or joints) and
cramp lightly using a slow-setting
epoxy glue.

● Mark out the shape of the top on
the dressed surface and cut

roughly to size.

● Gauge the desk to a thickness of
40mm and plane to thickness.

● Dress the edge of the top to the
profile line. Mark out the splays on
the edge and plane.

● Fit the loose tongues in the top
edge of the pedestals. Place the top
on the finished pedestals and move
each pedestal into its correct
position relative to the desk top.
Mark the position of the loose
tongues on to the underside of the
top. Remove the top and, using a
straight bit in a router, cut 30mm
deep trenches to receive the
splines.

● Sand the faces and edges of the
top to a final finish.

## Making the front and back rails and the drawer

• The front and back rails are cut from rosewood, are similar in shape, and are curved to follow the outer edge of the desk top. It will be necessary to shape this curve before marking and cutting the arch in each rail. The maximum width of each rail is 75mm, but they will need to be more than 90mm thick to allow for the curved shape to be cut. The rails are to finish at 50mm thick.

• The front rail will later be cut into two sections. The left half will form the front of the drawer, while the right half has two 100mm x 20mm loose tongues on the edge to fit trenches on the underside of the desk top, and a 35mm long tenon to fit the mortice in the pedestal.

• The back rail has four loose tongues, identical in size to those used in the front rail, securing it to the underside of the desk top. A tenon 35mm long on either end fits into the mortices cut in the pedestals.

• After cutting and fitting these joints, assemble the front rail in its final position and mark the position of the front of the drawer on the underside of the desk top. These lines will provide the basis for a working rod of the drawer which can be drawn on the underside of the desk top. Mark the two sides of the drawer at 90° to the longitudinal centre line of the desk top on the working rod, and mark the position of the drawer back at 90° to the drawer side to give a drawer length of 400mm. Cut the 300mm length from the front rail to form the drawer front.

• The drawer sides and runners are made from tallowwood, but any dense timber could be used. Prepare the drawer sides to sectional size 60mm x 19mm and cut to lengths marked from the working rod. Prepare the drawer back to sectional size

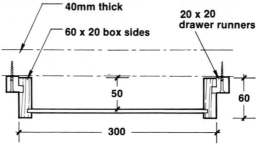

Fig 3.6 Details of the drawer.

50mm x 15mm and cut to the length marked from the working rod.

• Cut the 3mm wide groove in the drawer side to fit the drawer base. Cut a 10mm x 10mm groove down the outside faces of the drawer sides to fit the drawer runners, as shown in Fig 3.6.

• Mark and cut the angled lapped dovetails on the front of the drawer and, with the joints assembled, place the components over the working rod and mark the position of the common dovetails on the drawer back and sides. Cut and fit the joints.

• Sand all surfaces and glue and assemble the drawer, clamping lightly until the glue is dry.

• Shape the drawer runners to the sectional size shown in Fig 3.6. Drill and countersink for screws to fix the runners to the underside of the desk top.

## Assembly and finishing

• Sand all surfaces to a final finish. Glue the back rail to the pedestals using a slow-setting epoxy. Glue and assemble the top to the pedestals and back rails using fox wedges. **To allow movement in the top, apply glue only to the mortice and tenons between the pedestals and the top and not to the shoulders between the tenons.** Glue and fit the front rail, cramping lightly until the glue has cured or set.

• Fit the drawer runners to the underside of the desk top and adjust to ensure the drawer is free-moving.

• Apply three coats of Danish oil to the pedestals, rails and drawer. The desk top is finished with a satin finish polyurethane.

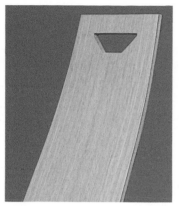

The view across the valley is of cypress trees and the rim of Kyneton township — coloured roofs on a dark green backdrop. The garden before you has a sparse precision reflecting the angularity of the house at your back. David Emery's home sits into the hillside, large intersecting faces of red brick and glass with a slate roof, dark from the rain. Walking up the sloping lawn across a terrace through a window wall, you enter the dining room with the same angles repeated in oblique walls, lofted ceiling, mezzanine floor above and kitchen below. The sense of space is little affected by moving inside. There are only three tables and several simple chairs in that large area, all finely framed, leaving the space uncluttered and expansive. No matter where you turn in that room, the fields and sky beyond are visible. A dining table, a squat inverted square pyramid on legs of thick glass blades, is the only large piece of furniture visible. It seems to float in space above the grey slate floor. To see his home and that living room is to understand better the influences affecting David's work.

He admits, 'I suppose this house must have influenced me; you can't live in a house like this without appreciating angular shapes. At the time we decided to build a friend gave us a biography of William Morris, and in that book was a photograph of his "Red House" which we liked very much. I began to make sketches of a house similar to that photograph, but soon realised my limitations as an architect. I took my drawings to Ken Robinson, a local architect and friend, who miraculously converted my ideas into an entirely different design which incorporated all the features we wanted. That design process has fascinated me ever since.'

As we sit over lunch, analysing how this furniture was derived from the angularity of the house, he says, with characteristic humility, 'I'm not a woodworker, just a maker of furniture.' It's the designer speaking where the medium is secondary to the form. True, he works coincidentally in wood, as he complements wood with glass, stainless steel, plastic laminates and leather when appropriate. He uses wood with a mechanical precision which denies its organic origins, finished with a gloss surface which would rival that found on the bonnet of a Rolls-Royce.

In his showroom, an old shop front facing the main street of sleepy Kyneton, a replica of that pyramidal table from his living room looks much less comfortable. Even so, with its perfectly matched silver ash veneered top and clear glass slabs as legs, it levitates mysteriously. Adjacent is an oval table made by a friend, an interesting shape finished in grey epoxy over MDF board. The contrast in tables is in warmth and softness, characters given to David's table by the honey-coloured glow of the silver ash. David remains unconvinced that timber is a critical element of his work, even though his success has been its mastery, making it compliant to geometric shapes alien to its original characteristics. His veneers bend over amazingly sharp curves around the edge of tables, a technique he has perfected with his vacuum press.

Large geometrical shapes are his forte, usually made in hollow form construction from MDF board. Although he claims to have little knowledge of mathematics, he has an unquestioned ability in spatial relationships. Intersecting oblique planes are a joy to him. His hollow form table tops have numerous internal ribs to ensure the surface remains true, and concealed mounting plates for the massive glass blades. The intersection of these internal elements would be enough to make most woodworkers blanch. Strangely, he does not see himself as a designer, but his ability to solve complex problems of shape, form and structure suggests otherwise. He says, 'I don't venerate wood, just use it,' but he does so in a different way from most. To deny dominance of a medium is not to deny the craft he uses or the art he employs. 'I do know something about proportion,' is one of his most masterly understatements.

**Bowl, 700mm diameter x 110mm, MDF lacquered with veneered rim, chrome lip and stand.**
Photographer: Justine Noy.

Many woodworkers are wary of working with architects, principally because they see themselves as designers and believe there is a potential conflict of purpose in working together.

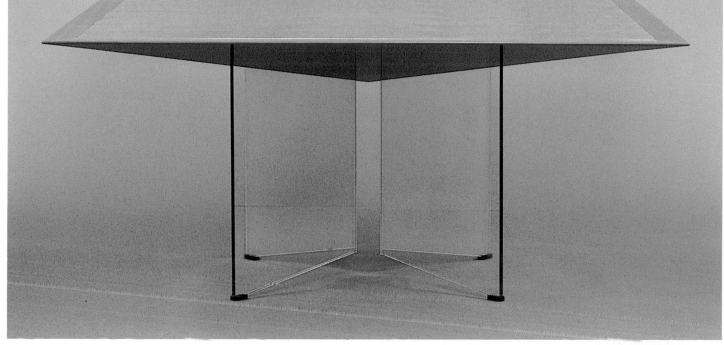

Dining table, 1500 x 1500
x 720, blister sapele
veneer on hollow-core
MDF top, 12mm glass
legs and chrome inlay.
Photographer: John
Brash.

More likely it is a clash of professional wills or vanities which is the problem in such a partnership. David Emery's natural humility serves him well in this regard, as he is willing to make whatever an architect might design. 'The best working relationships I have are with architects who accept that I have a contribution to make and are willing to consult on detailing and materials. I just like making things, and any opportunity to work with any architect or designer I accept willingly. It's a partnership. I've yet to make any commission like this without making some decisions of my own or designing some detail.'

His constant refinements of techniques used in working complex angular shapes has brought him many architectural commissions for fittings and furniture. His ability to handle these complex constructions has provided opportunities to experiment with different edge treatments for acutely angled surfaces using veneers and laminates. On the wall in his workshop were the drawings for an architect-designed reception unit for the Melbourne City Council. It resembled the maze of lines usually presented as problems on oblique planes when studying descriptive geometry. David finds excitement in solving the problems he encounters in translating those simple design drawings into finely crafted timber and laminate.

His career in wood began in 1974, when as a public servant he saw frustration and lack of fulfilment as his future.

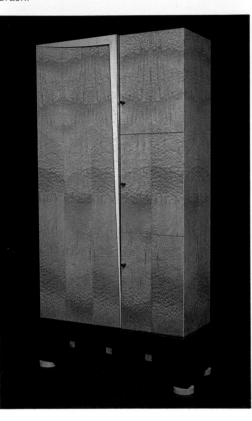

Cabinet, 2000 x 1000 x 420, blister sapele and ebonised poplar veneer on MDF beech feet.
Photographer: John Brash.

He resigned, and without any great knowledge or skills accepted a commission to make some furniture for a friend's restaurant. He opened his showroom and workshop in a disused store on the outskirts of Kyneton in 1975, relying on the passing trade provided by the Calder Highway to buy the adzed Oregon furniture he made. It was a storm, however, which marked a change in direction. In 1976 many elm trees were blown down in a violent thunderstorm. This *free* timber prompted a search for designs of domestic furniture suited to elm. He travelled to England to study some of the traditional methods of working this timber and returned with a different intent, realising that traditional furniture was not the best solution for his small workshop. Instead he designed tables and chairs with clean simple lines, and in 1978 he made a number of tables which had a rounded leg at each corner intruding into the top. It was a photograph of one of these tables which caught the eye of architect Aldo Giurgola in 1985, and David was invited to make the furniture for the Speaker's suite in the New Parliament House in Canberra. He recollects, 'I was a bit disappointed that it was this table which interested them, because in the interim I had developed my pyramidal table and was off on a new venture using hollow forms. The opportunity of working with Aldo and the supervising architect Geoffrey Siebens was one of the great experiences in my life.'

As for other craftsmen who worked on the furniture and fittings in the New Parliament House, the experience provided some larger commissions and a new clientele. The Speaker's table was a complex commission, and the professional concern shown by Aldo Giurgola for the most minute details of design astounded David. He was telephoned by Aldo from New York on several occasions to discuss details raised weeks before. David gained a greater respect for the professionalism of architects of that stature, which in turn introduced a new self-discipline to his own work.

The year he was introduced to Aldo Giurgola provided another valuable experience. David spent 1985 as workshop manager for the Meat Market in Melbourne, a craft co-operative which derived its name from the old meat hall in North Melbourne now used as a showroom and workshop for all crafts. David relates, 'I displayed the first of my inverted square pyramid tables at its Easter Survey Show and gained a commission to make three tables for the boardroom of the Institute of Architects. That contract brought other work for architects, and I was given a commission to fit out the corporate offices for an advertising agency. My contact with different architects in Melbourne has continued ever since.

'Recently I placed one of my tables in a retail furniture store in Melbourne, and I'm hopeful that I can develop this as an outlet. I have grave doubts about relying on galleries, as people come to exhibitions to look, not to buy. The success of this venture is still to be proved, but the owner of the store is confident. For it to earn its place on the showroom floor, however, my product must hold its own against that of larger manufacturers, as I can be treated no differently from them.

'I don't think there's a problem in selling if your design is what the public want. Woodworkers and furniture makers keep thinking that everyone is as excited about our furniture as we are ourselves, and they're not. It's sensible to remind yourself continually that the market is very small. It's nonsense to think, "There must be thousands of people waiting to buy my furniture if only I could reach them". True, the public isn't well-informed about "designer" furniture, or commercial furniture for that matter. It gets almost no coverage in the media, and even if we had the finances to change that situation I doubt if the limited production capacity of "craft" producers could pay for the time and money spent in promotion. I'm not interested in operating a company employing many people to make my designs in furniture. I like best working by myself, with help at odd times, making what I enjoy making.'

**Bistro table, top dark and light brush box and silver ash veneers, legs blue lacquered steel.**
Photographer: John Brash.

In 1991 David enrolled in a postgraduate design course at the Melbourne Institute of Technology to learn more about the design process that fascinated him with the building of his house. He has earned recognition as a designer of note in Australia. What wonders will he create when he becomes qualified in his craft? No doubt his humility will be retained, as will that fascination for 'planes in space' which gives timber in his designs a different dimension to that envisioned by most woodworkers.

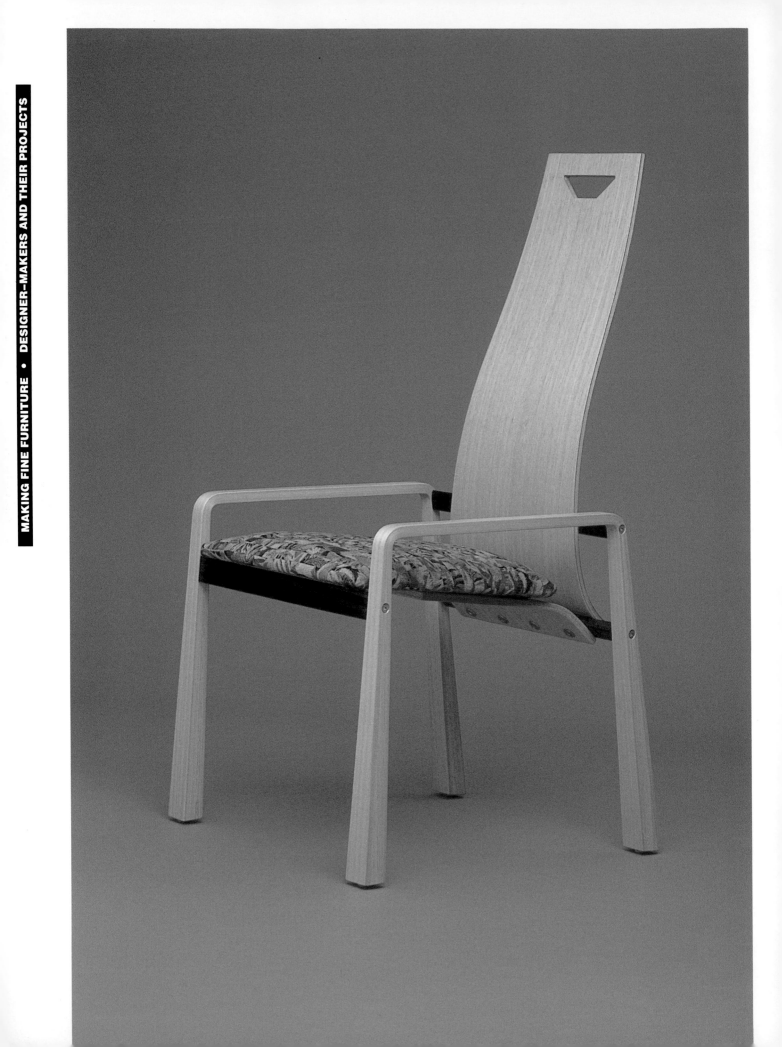

# Whistler Chair

ost woodworkers make chairs from solid timber. Often it limits the shape and structure of the piece, as a solid member is only as strong as its weakest part. This compels a designer to use a factor of safety which ensures the member is thicker and wider than it need be if localised weaknesses are not considered. The Whistler chair has a form made possible by lamination, a simple process used far more by industry than by designer-makers. It allows members to be used which are thinner in section than those found in chairs made from solid timber. Jointing is not necessary as members can be held together with screws or metal fittings. For this reason a laminated chair is light yet strong, with members which can curve to form a firm composite of opposing shapes and angles.

If the profiles and relationship of the components shown in the side view of Fig 4.2 are not altered, the construction described here could be use to produce a wide variety of chairs of different shape and style. All that need be altered is the shape of the individual members shown in the front view. The simplicity of David Emery's Whistler chair makes adaption uncomplicated. As making the formers used to cramp the laminates to shape is a significant task in making a laminated chair, the process lends itself to small production runs in a workshop rather than one-off designs.

**Whistler chair**
**© David Emery.**
Photographer: John Brash.

## Making the chair

The chair is composed of eight members plus fittings and an upholstered seat cushion. There are two leg frames which are mirror

**Fig 4.1 Anatomy of the Whistler chair.**

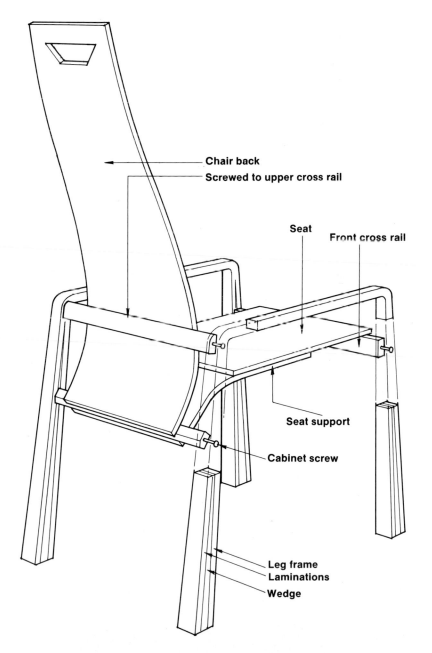

Chair back
Screwed to upper cross rail

Seat
Front cross rail

Seat support

Cabinet screw

Leg frame
Laminations
Wedge

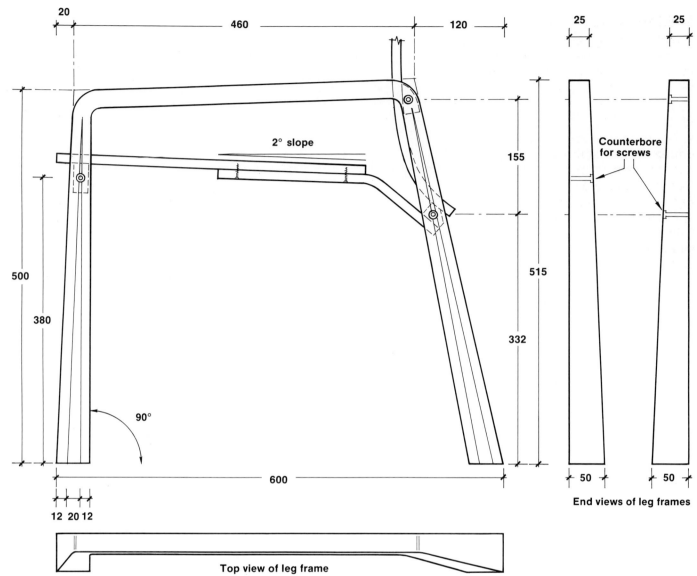

2° slope

**Counterbore for screws**

**End views of leg frames**

**Top view of leg frame**

**Fig 4.2 Construction details of the chair.**

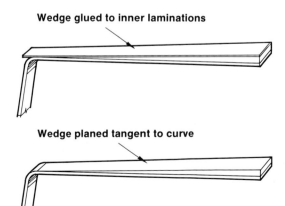

**Wedge glued to inner laminations**

**Wedge planed tangent to curve**

**Fig 4.3 Method of forming the leg frames with laminations and wedges.**

32

images of each other; a seat from flat 12mm ply; a seat support which is purpose-formed; a laminated backrest and three cross rails. The members are assembled using metal fittings, but the cross rails are glued to the backrest to give the chair lateral rigidity.

It is necessary to make a working rod of the side view of the chair on a sheet of plywood. This working rod will show the critical relationship between components and give a reference when making the formers for the laminated components. A full-size front view may be helpful but is not critical, as each cross rail is identical in length and the inside face of both leg frames is vertical.

## Making the leg frames

● Make a former shaped to the inside of the leg frame as shown on the working rod. This former can be of scrap timber, and is glued and screwed to the face of an MDF or plywood board.

● The right and left leg frames differ only in that the angled face and the counterboring of the fixture holes are on opposite sides. Each frame is made from approximately 40 laminations of 0.6mm veneer, cut 70mm wide to allow for trimming and shaping, and two timber wedges. The legs are made up in three stages.

● Half the laminates are glued and pressed over the former. A glue with a pot life of up to two hours, such as urea formaldahyde, should be used. (Other glues with an extended working time would also be suitable.) Leave the laminates cramped in the former until the glue is dry.

● Cut wedge-shaped inserts 70mm wide and tapering from 20mm to 2mm and glue to the outside of the laminations, using a faster-setting glue. When dry the outer face is dressed until the thick end of the wedge is 18mm thick and the thin end is tangent to the curve of the laminations, as shown in Fig 4.3.

● The leg frame is then placed back on the former and the remaining laminations glued and cramped to the outside face. Allow the glue to dry.

● Final shaping is done using a combination of machine planing, sawing and hand planing.

● The position of the counterbored holes for the fixing screws should be marked on the leg frames from the working rod. For counterboring, use a bit which will produce a flat-bottomed hole. Do **not** use a fitting screw with a countersink-shaped head as the wedging action of this head may split the laminates when tightened. A modern cabinet screw or a

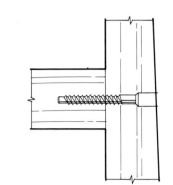

**Cabinet screw**

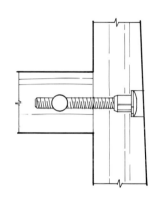

**Knock-down fitting**
**connector bolt and brass cross dowel**

Fig 4.4 Alternative methods of joining the leg frames to the cross rails.

knock-down fitting of connector bolt and brass cross dowel, as shown in Fig 4.4, would be suitable to fix the leg frames to the cross rails. Do **not** use a conventional woodscrew for this purpose as it would be screwing into end grain.

## Making the cross rails

● Prepare the timber to size for the three cross rails 40mm x 20mm, and cut to a length of 450mm. The back rails are to be shaped as detailed on the working rod. A dense strong timber should be used for the cross rails, and David Emery chose one of contrasting colour to that used in making the laminates.

● Drill the holes in the ends of each cross rail to suit the type of fitting being used.

## Making the seat and seat support

• The seat is made from a flat section of 12mm ply, shaped and upholstered as preferred. As shown on the drawing, it is shaped from a 450mm x 420mm rectangle. The seat and seat support can be made in one unit, but this makes the upholstery and the pre-stressing of the legs during assembly more complex tasks.

• The seat support is purpose-formed around a former made to the shape shown on the working rod. Screws are used to joint the seat to the front rail and the seat

support, and the seat support to the back cross rail.

## Making the chair back

• Make a male and female former to match the curve of the back shown on the working rod. To ensure that the formers do not deform under pressure, they should be made from a close-grained, strong timber. If you have access to a vacuum press, or have a small air compressor and can make a simple vacuum press, only one former will be required to press the laminates.

• As the curves in the back are not

**Fig 4.5 Contour and shape of the chair back.**

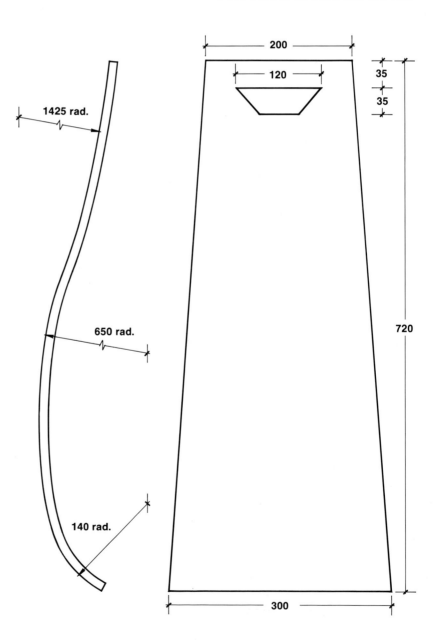

tight, 1mm thick veneers can be used. Alternating the grain directions in the laminates will produce an undesirable ply effect on the edges of the chair back. Eleven 1mm veneers are cut to size, with the grain running vertically on the back. Two 0.6mm veneers of contrasting colour are cut with grain running across the back. These are placed near the front and back faces to give the necessary resistance to cupping.

• When the laminates have been glued, cut the back to shape, as shown in Fig 4.5. The hand grip at the top is optional or can be shaped to reflect an element adjacent to where the chair is to be used.

• The rear cross rails are to be glued to the back. Small biscuits would be ideal to align these members and strengthen the joint, but short dowels or a small spline could be used. Assemble the chair and mark the position of the cross rails on to the back. Cut the slots for the biscuits and check the accuracy of their positioning by reassembling the chair and checking the original setting out.

## Finishing and assembly

• Glue the back to the two back rails and cramp lightly.

• Assemble the leg frames to the cross rails using the fixing screws.

• Screw the seat to the front rail, and the seat support to the lower back rail.

• It is necessary to pre-stress the laminates in the leg frames. A bent lamination is at its weakest when the applied force is tending to straighten the member. This stress can separate the laminates. To pre-stress the frames, nail parallel cleats to a surface, the distance between them being 3mm or 4mm less than that between the outer surfaces of the front and back leg. Spring the legs between the cleats and screw the seat support to the underside of the seat. This will be sufficient to ensure that the laminations are always stressed in the direction of their greatest rather than their least resistance.

• Disassemble the chair, fine sand all surfaces and apply the finish. Reassemble the chair and fit the upholstered seat cushion.

 Kevin Perkins reversed the utility truck out of the carport and followed the track around a giant gum, past timber stacks and storage sheds, then on to a dirt road and we were off snaking into the Huon Valley far below. He lives atop a mountain in a workshop-cum-house, its weathered timbers backed by giant blue gums above the mountain's rim. A Cape Barron Goose weather vane was perched on the peak of a gable, while its many carved cousins had alighted on others. Across the valley, hills were mist-blue and timbered, ridge on ridge. We turned the final corner on to the highway and headed down the valley in the afternoon light, south and then west to Farmhouse Creek. Kevin was to show me something of the south-west and a stand of Huon pine. Leaving the orchards behind, we passed scattered settlements, homes for timber workers, as open fields gave way to forest.

Farmhouse Creek is famous in Australia as the site of one of the more violent confrontations between protesters, loggers and the police in a protracted battle which featured nightly on national TV in the late 1980s. That afternoon the creek looked rain-drenched and peaceful, but the logging scars on the hillside remain and recent wounds suggest that either the battle was won by the loggers or a studied truce has ensued. We stopped the truck in a particularly embattled area, the site of clear felling where regrowth has begun, and set off on foot to follow an old logging trail, badly scarred by run-off, which angles across a slope toward the creek below. A number of large Huon pines were on the creek edge, moss hanging thickly from their lower branches. They had a fine textured grey bark and these specimens, although 1500-2000 years old, were but small trees. They are so precious that if others knew of them they would not survive, for tree poaching is a profitable pastime in these parts and Huon pine of whatever size is a prize worth the risk.

How you view those few survivors of a vanquished species depends upon your knowledge, perception and experience. We see as we are. In the 1960s, people who hugged trees and regarded them as wonders of nature and worthy of protection were considered eccentric. Most people now recognise that the

**Incised decoration with carved leaves bound with copper on a celery top post in the home of Kevin Perkins.**
Photographer: Deborah Taylor.

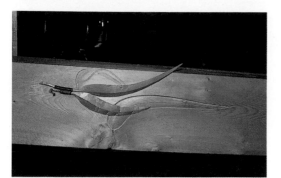

**Table, *Dining at the Coast - Clouds and Seagull*, sassafras and ebony, photographed in Kevin Perkins' workshop.**
Photographer: Uffe Schulze.

future of mankind may well depend on the persistence and courage of such eccentrics. Public attitudes are changing, but whether at a pace to direct political will and match commercial influence is yet to be proven. The people in Tasmania have much riding on that public contest. There are those, like Kevin Perkins, who have a public position on this contest and a viewpoint derived from witnessing shortsighted industrial development destroying much of what he values.

Tasmanian timbers have been valued for two centuries for their beauty and durability. Until recently, the latter characteristic was pre-eminent in merchants' minds as Huon pine was sold worldwide for everything from paving blocks to piles. That it is a magnificent cabinet timber, extremely slow-growing and a finite resource, was hardly considered at all. Public perception changed in the early 1970s as the conservation movement gained a voice. At that time a strange, but not unusually stupid, decision by the Tasmanian Hydro-Electricity Commission marked a significant shift in the career

of Kevin Perkins. The Gordon River was to be dammed for hydro-electric generation and the magnificent Lake Peddar in the South-West Wilderness flooded. The flooding caused a public outcry, but despite this a policy decision was made to flood the valley without first recovering the trees below the proposed water level. Huon pines and Tasmanian myrtles would be lost forever. What followed was a salvage operation set against the rising waters behind the dam.

The climate in the mid-1970s was right to challenge people's perceptions of *modern* materials and *modern* furniture. The contemporary practice was for timber mills to convert forest giants into thin, narrow boards for use in furniture. Kevin Perkins recalls the period: 'At that time, dining table tops were made from solid wood which looked like panels of narrow flooring boards glued together. I hoped that by designing and making furniture which used whole solid sections of trees, I could provide the Tasmanian public with an alternative to manufactured synthetic/plastic and those narrow boards. I hoped as well that the salvage operators working to retrieve the timber from Lake Peddar would have a commercial reason to retrieve the stump/root and T-fork sections with the butt logs. It worked, and those forest oddments, which had previously been burnt, I later made into "sculptured tables" in which the top was from giant flitches and the legs from natural forked logs . . .' Most of the craft timber removed from Lake Peddar appeared in furniture as panels with stirring colour and grain. Kevin Perkins was able to explore the refracted light and colour in that timber with dramatic effect.

Some of the craft timber from Lake Peddar was used in furniture and panelling for the New Parliament House in the national capital, Canberra. Those craftsmen fortunate enough to work on that magnificent building consider the experience as the high point in their career. Kevin Perkins was initially commissioned to design and make timber panelling for the Prime Minister's office. Doors and jambs were added to the commission, and he was later asked to submit design sketches for the Prime Minister's furniture, which he was also asked to make. What began as a single commission grew to almost four years of frenzied work. Aldo Giurgola, the principal architect for the New Parliament House, soon realised that not only was Kevin Perkins a master designer-maker but that he had a forester's knowledge and an amazing range of quality Tasmanian timbers at his disposal. That Huon pine taken from the hillsides around Lake Peddar was used to panel the walls of the Prime Minister's suite. 'It was a written brief for panelling, and the first images which came to me were of conventional frames infilled with timber panels. But when you looked at the matched flitches taken from whole logs of Huon pine, it

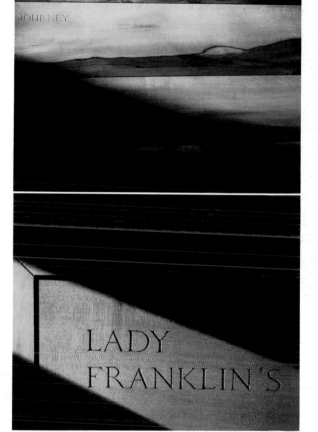

**Detail of Landscape Series table —** *Lady Franklin's Journey 1842.* Photographer: Uffe Schulze.

**Corner detail Landscape Series table —** *Lady Franklin's Journey 1842.* Photographer: Uffe Schulze.

**Interior of the home of Kevin Perkins.**
Photographer: Deborah Taylor.

**TV cabinet, galvanised sheet steel, celery top pine, satin sycamore and melamine. 209mm x 133mm x 53mm.**
Photographer: Uffe Schulze.

**Detail of TV cabinet.**
Photographer: Uffe Schulze.

seemed criminal to cut them. We devised a method of fixing them ''freestanding'' against the wall. We were even able to leave waney edges on some of the niche ''panels'' which represented the breaking apart of old bark on smooth barked trees, revealing fresh, virginal bark. The credenza doors had naturally imposed bends, much like bending back the corners on a piece of paper, which carried this new bark notion further.' Those panels of glowing timber have been among the most photographed surfaces in the New Parliament House.

Kevin Perkins is a designer who works sympathetically with each piece of timber and with an eye for all things natural. To achieve this, you must search patiently through timber stacks for a 'stick' with just the right characteristics. There are many stacks for Kevin to search through in his shed, yard and workshop, the latter racked with planks from floor to ceiling. Here table tops stand on edge ready for inspiration or the time to add legs. Past ideas, heavy with dust, hang from rafters or clutter corners. Yet there is an unusual order to it all, possibly

because his home shares a common wall with the workshop. His skills are displayed on the walls and fittings of every room in his home. A bird's head emerges from a post as if rising from water. Incised cryptic messages and animal forms catch the light on posts and panels; a leaf and gum nuts are relief carved into a beam, and the head of an echidna peeps over the top of a high-backed chair. Kevin Perkins is undoubtedly an artist with the economy of a cartoonist, for five incised lines in a post define the neck and head of a bird with remarkable clarity.

**Goose bench, Huon pine.**
Photographer: Uffe Schulze.

Although much of his work is in solid timber, he works with 3mm veneers for large surfaces such as table tops. My favourite amongst his veneered 'story tables' is entitled *Lady Franklin's Journey*. They are all simple rectangular tables, with the intrigue coming from the pattern and message they convey. Kevin explains, 'I slice off consecutive layers from a baulk of figured timber. In the case of the *Abel Tasman*, it was blackheart sassafras, which has deep brown figures on a yellow straw background. Each successive layer reminded me of a receding shore line, and when I placed them beneath each other they suggested the south-west coastline of Tasmania, progressively changing and fading as Tasman first saw it in 1642. Another

**Detail of credenza cabinet, shelves and door openings. Huon pine and Tasmanian myrtle, Prime Minister's office furniture, New Parliament House, Canberra.**
Photograph courtesy of MGT Architects.

**Corner detail of Prime Minister's desk Tasmanian myrtle, West Australian jarrah, end grain jarrah stripping, and burl myrtle corner detail.**
Photograph courtesy of MGT Architects.

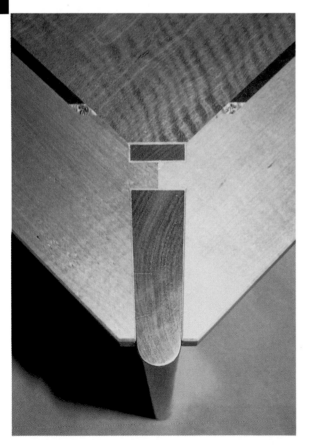

travel table depicts the overland journey of Lady Franklin from Hobart to the west coast in 1842. Her epic journey is represented in the unique natural staining of the spalted sassafras timber, which to me represents the mountains, valleys and finally the coastline that Lady Franklin encountered as she travelled. When I cut into timber like this, it's like opening a Pandora's box of possibilities. Every piece suggests something different to me, a different picture or a story.' Each panel is thicknessed and edge-glued before gluing the large panel to a core. The words *Lady Franklin's* are incise carved into the left-hand corner of the first panel, *Journey* into the second, and the year *1842* into the right corner of the last panel. As with most of his work, the economy of expression and the simplicity of the table makes the work dynamic and compelling.

Unlike most of the craftsmen in this book, Kevin Perkins had a conventional trade training, working as a joiner in the days when windows and doors were measured and made in the workshop. The advent of aluminium extrusions and off-the-shelf joinery had such an unfortunate impact on the trade that he resigned as head lecturer at the Hobart Technical College and sought a new direction. In 1978 he used a $2000 grant to prepare an exhibition which was a scll-out success, and since then has worked on commissions for clients throughout

Australia. His national credentials for fine design, exquisite precision and knowledge of Tasmanian timbers have given him wide public recognition. His casual manner is deceptive, as he speaks with authority and conviction. Ask a question, and you get a direct answer delivered with fixed eyes and slow smile. The answers are practised — the questions you ask have obviously been addressed many times before, but the answers are presented with a sincerity which has gained him the respect of business and government in Tasmania.

He joined with others in making submissions to the Helsham Inquiry, established by the Tasmanian government to make recommendations on a path through the political minefield of forest management in the state. As a consequence, Kevin is involved in three projects which aim at adding value to Tasmania's forest products. The most adventurous of these continues his involvement with the Hobart School of Art, where he has lectured for many years. This prestigious school has established a postgraduate course in Wood Design (Furniture for Production), with an objective of providing the furniture industry of Tasmania with a prototype design facility where students can work with Kevin and others in developing designs for manufacturers. This Centre for Furniture Design is unique in Australia, and Kevin Perkins is currently working with companies on new designs and the modification of designs currently in production.

In 1989 Aldo Giurgola designed the Saint Thomas Aquinas Parish Church in a suburb of Canberra and invited Kevin to design and make furniture. The pews are in Tasmanian oak and the altar, lectern and baptismal font in Huon pine. The 90 pews were joined with knock-down fittings and were sanded, oiled and assembled by the parishioners. He admits that large-scale projects like this give him a great deal of satisfaction: 'If I have a talent, it's for interpreting written briefs quickly and accurately assessing work schedules. I like working with architects like Aldo who give you a lot to contribute. Parishioners make good clients because they want your designs to be a symbolic part of *their* church. They are really appreciative of your work.'

There are few craftspersons in Australia with a better, more intuitive feel for their medium than Kevin Perkins. To know timber, to have the stockpiles and suppliers which make careful selection possible, is only part of his magic. He has the ability to put it all together with a romantic imagination directing the design. There is nothing conformist about his furniture, whether compositions of angular surfaces or organic shapes — his mastery of proportion and use of subtle decorative detail gives each piece an unusual character, a character easily identified as the signature of Tasmania's most outstanding woodworker.

**Corner detail of oval side table, Tasmanian myrtle with flame myrtle table top insert, Prime Minister's office furniture, New Parliament House, Canberra.**
Photograph courtesy of MGT Architects.

procedure used in general cabinetmaking. To ensure that the lengths of components are marked accurately, a working rod should be drawn on a sheet of plywood of the front view shown in Fig 5.1 — it can also assist when gluing and assembling the carcase to check whether it is true.

Bird's-eye Huon pine veneers are used for the face of the doors. This is an unusual timber and could be difficult to acquire, but any highly figured, close-grained yellow-coloured timber could be used. Similarly, the locking stiles and outer edges of the doors and the inlay on the front edge of the shelves are in sycamore, which is green in colour with an amber flare caused by prominent medullary rays. Any timber which has a similar blend of colours could be used. The surface of each door is divided into panels by a 4mm wide inlay strip of jarrah. This timber is also used in a 3mm wide insert between the beading and door frame and as an edging on one of the door locking stiles — it is a dense-grained hardwood with a deep rich red colour, bordering on purple.

## Making the carcase

- Prepare the timber for the sides, top mitred panels and the base in boards 405mm x 21mm. Cut a 12mm x 12mm rebate on one edge to receive the back panel. Cut each to length after measuring from the working rod, allowing end waste for the dovetail joints between the base and sides.

- Mark out and cut the common stepped dovetail joints. Mark the position for the two fixed shelves and drill and countersink for the screws used to fix the shelves to the sides. Cut the recesses to take the 15mm x 15mm plugs to cover the screw heads.

- Cut the mitres on the ends of the remaining boards and align the joints with biscuits using a plate joiner.

- Sand all surfaces on each member to a fine finish and glue the top centre mitre joint and cramp lightly. Check for square

and brace the joint with short battens. Leave to dry.

- Glue and assemble the remaining joints and assemble the carcase, cramp lightly and check for true.

- Prepare the two fixed shelves to sectional size 375mm x 21mm. Glue 12mm x 3mm sycamore strips in the front edges and cut shelves to a length of 958mm, or to fit the cabinet.

- Remove the waste from the dovetails and fine sand all surfaces. Screw fixed shelves in the carcase and plug with 15mm x 15mm end grain Huon pine.

- Prepare a back panel from 12mm thick solid timber. Here two boards only were edge-glued, but veneered plywood or customwood could be used. Cut the panel to fit the opening and trim to fit. Secure the panel by pinning (if solid timber is used, do not glue).

- Cut the adjustable shelves to size from 21mm thick customwood or ply and glue a 3mm edging to replicate that on the fixed shelves.

## Making the doors

- Cut the 12mm marine ply for the door panels to shape and edge the top and outer edges with 3mm thick sycamore strips.

- Prepare the sycamore locking stiles to sectional size of 33mm x 18mm. (One stile is to be edged with a 3mm thick strip of jarrah and reduced to 33mm wide.)

- Cut and fit the mitre joints on either end of the locking stile and the door panels. Align the joint with biscuits using a plate jointer. Glue and assemble the joint.

- Trim the lower end of the sycamore locking stile to form a flush surface with the 12mm marine ply door panel. This allows the Huon pine veneers to cover this mitre joint, retaining the semi-circular shape of the lower part of the door uninterrupted. Check the

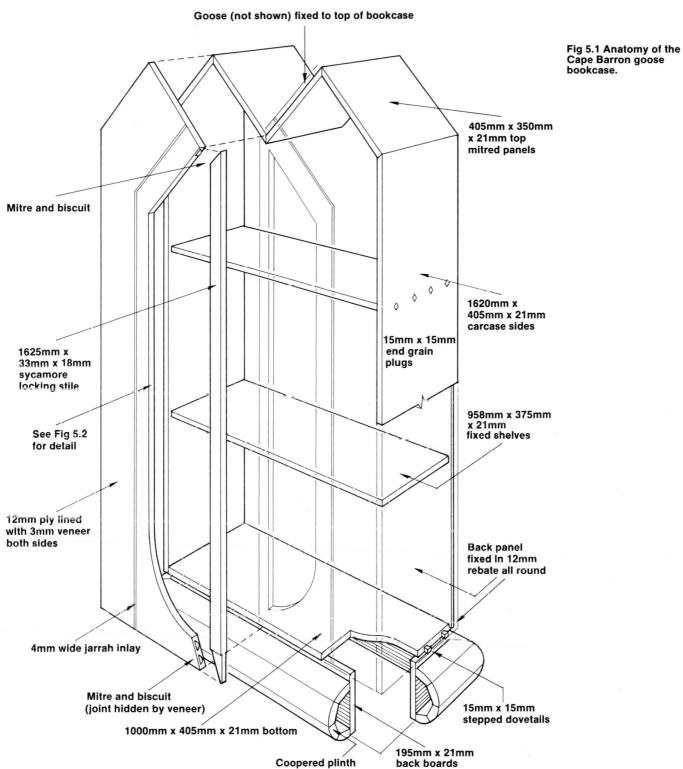

Goose (not shown) fixed to top of bookcase

Fig 5.1 Anatomy of the Cape Barron goose bookcase.

405mm x 350mm x 21mm top mitred panels

Mitre and biscuit

1620mm x 405mm x 21mm carcase sides

15mm x 15mm end grain plugs

1625mm x 33mm x 18mm sycamore locking stile

See Fig 5.2 for detail

958mm x 375mm x 21mm fixed shelves

12mm ply lined with 3mm veneer both sides

Back panel fixed in 12mm rebate all round

4mm wide jarrah inlay

Mitre and biscuit (joint hidden by veneer)

1000mm x 405mm x 21mm bottom

Coopered plinth

15mm x 15mm stepped dovetails

195mm x 21mm back boards

shape of the doors against the carcase and trim to fit.

• Glue the 3mm thick Huon pine veneers to front and back faces of door panels. (If commercial veneers of lesser thickness are used, thicker ply panels will be needed to give a finished door thickness of 18mm.) Trim the veneer flush with the edges.

• Cut the 4mm wide trench for the jarrah inlay in the face of the door panels. Glue the veneer inlay and dress flush.

• Glue a 3mm thick jarrah strip to the edges of the locking stiles and door panels to frame the glass panels, as shown in Fig 5.2, and trim flush with door faces.

• Cut the 7mm sycamore quadrant mould for the glass panels to size and glue flush with the front face of the doors.

• Cut and fit the 3mm sycamore quadrant mould for the inside face of the door.

**Fig 5.2 Detailed dimensions and structure of the Cape Barron goose bookcase.**

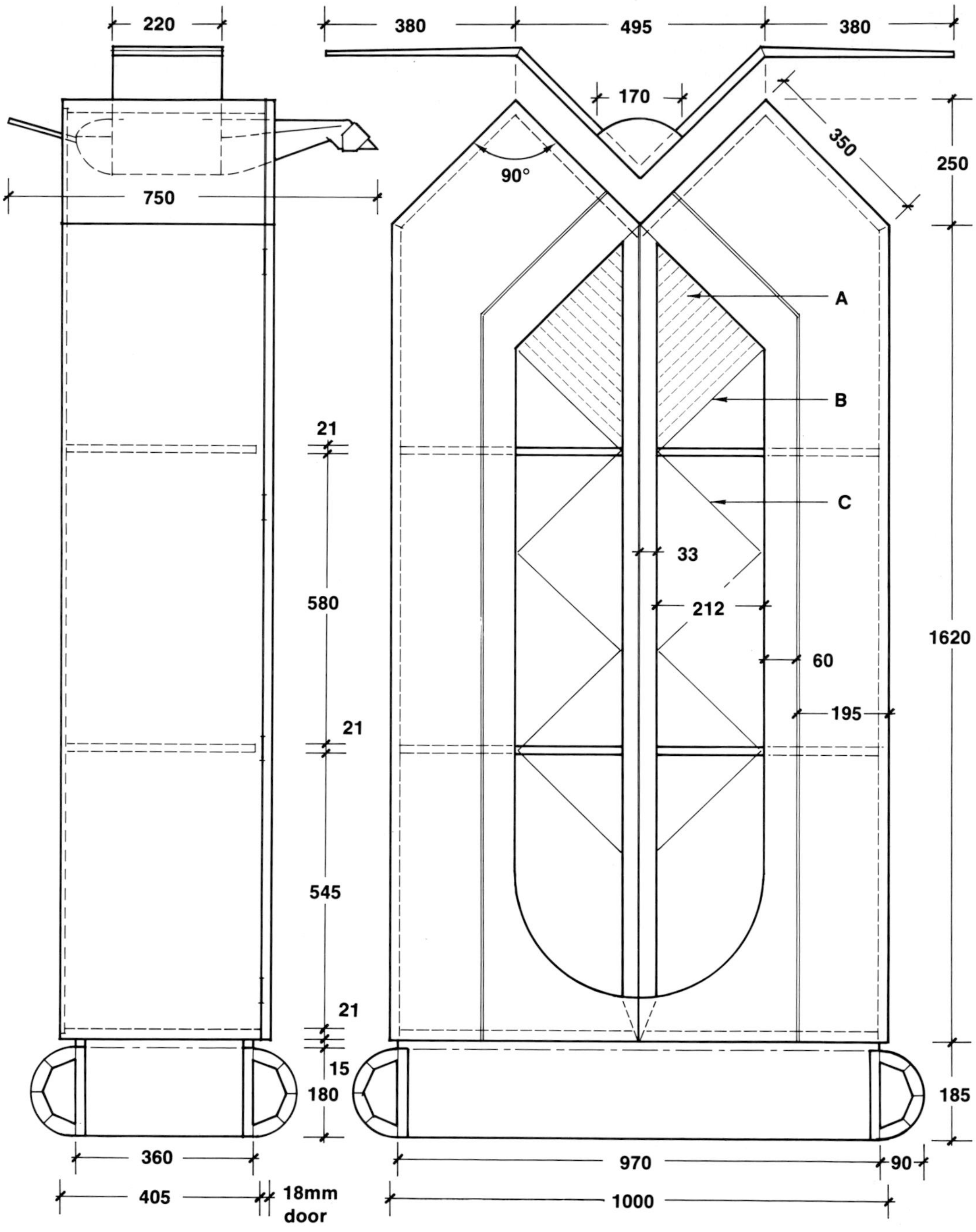

A — wire reinforced glass
B — bevelled edges and silicon mastic bead
C — sandblasted groove

- Fit the four 50mm brass hinges to each door.

- Fine sand all surfaces and fit the lock in the locking stile. Hinge the doors to the carcase.

## Plinth

- The plinth is coopered from four sections of sycamore, edge-glued with biscuits and planed to a 180mm diameter semi-circular shape. Prepare the coopered shape in two 1700mm lengths.

- Cut the coopered section to approximate lengths for the front, back and two side sections of the plinth and glue to a 195mm x 21mm backboard as shown in Fig 5.1.

- Cut the mitres on either end of each section and glue the plinth together.

- Fine sand all surfaces. Apply an ebony stain to the top edge of the plinth to give a shadow line, and fix the plinth to the base of the carcase.

## Cape Barron goose

- Shape the body and tail of the bird in Huon pine and shape the beak from ebony to fit the head (*see* detail in Fig 5.1).

- Prepare the timber for the wings to sectional size of 220mm x 20mm and cut to lengths of 2mm x 400mm and 2mm x 350mm, tapering the wing tips to 10mm thick. Cut the mitre joints and align and strengthen with biscuits. Glue the joints.

- Drill the holes in the wings and the carcase for two 12mm diameter brass pins to fix the bird to the carcase.

- Drill holes for two screws to fix the tail to the body of the bird.

- Fine sand all components. Glue the wings and beak to the body and screw the tail to the bird.

## Finishing and fitting glass panels

- The finish used was a

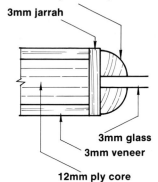

7mm sycamore quadrant
3mm jarrah
3mm glass
3mm veneer
12mm ply core

Fig 5.3 Details of the door structure and glazing.

commercial shellac-based spirit finish. Care should be taken to select a finish which will not significantly darken or change the colour of the timbers used.

- Each glass panel is in two sections. The top triangular-shaped section in each door is cut from 3mm polished wire-reinforced glass. The lower section is cut from 3mm window glass in which a pattern of 2.5mm wide grooves has been sandblasted. The edges which form the joint between these two sections of glass are bevelled and filled with a silicon mastic. Fit the glass panels and secure by pinning the interior quadrant mould in position.

DAVID
OWEN
TUCKER
1991

Thankfully, most television pro-
grammes and films made in
Australia now depict Australians as
urban dwellers. The image of the
Australian as bronzed and athletic
is largely a myth, for although the
climate and lifestyle provide
opportunities for the young to be
both, most people are sensible and
react to the heat by sitting in the
shade. Perhaps the young people
who came to the north coast of New South Wales in the 1970s
came to act out the good life as perceived from the comfort of
their urban living room. Most were ill-equipped with skills and
knowledge to undertake a new life in what they hoped would
be an ideal wilderness. David Tucker and Robert Parker came
to Dundurrabin and stayed because they had found a 'place in
the bush'. It's odd that two of the most outstanding
woodworkers in this country should choose to settle in this
remote hamlet in the mountains west of the Dorrigo Plateau.
Neither had the intention of working in wood, and they came
for different reasons.

David Tucker spent most of his youth in North Africa and
Europe following the postings of his English father. An inspired
Welsh woodwork teacher at his final school left him with the
ambition to be a cabinetmaker, but on finishing school and
coming to Australia, he found this trade was not what he
imagined and accepted an apprenticeship in photo-engraving.
He shared a house with seven young people in Melbourne, all
living out the 'new age of love and understanding', and it was
decided that they would establish a settlement on the north
coast of New South Wales. They settled in Dundurrabin on the
edge of a wilderness, west of the Dorrigo Plateau and inland
from Coffs Harbour. David describes their first glimpse of the
Dorrigo Plateau: 'Mist was rising out of the trees, great rolling
clouds came up from the valley below and it felt like home.'

David selected a site and designed his cabin scaled to the
size of his yoga mat, with a bed loft above. He reflects, 'I built
the frame for my cabin on top of the hill and carried each piece
down to be erected on the site. As part of the fundamentalist
principles of the day, the frame was jointed and put together
with wooden dowels.' So began his new career as woodworker.
That cabin was photographed and appeared in a book on

David Tucker

51

alternative buildings of Australia. Looking at the now much-extended home, which incorporates that original cabin, it is possible to imagine that David might have been an architect.

Sitting on the terrace of his home above the gulley, with the creek running noisily below and blue gums growing tall amongst scrub on the far hillside, you are at peace. A Mozart sonata drifts through the bush, and the smell of coffee is in the air. This feels like the best of all possible worlds. David now has all the creative comforts of the city, electricity, telephone and TV, and is only one-and-a-half hours from the large inland city of Armidale, with its university, shops and schools. He reacts directly to my assertion that he has forsaken the original objectives of the good life. 'The purpose in coming here wasn't regressive, to return to an earlier age or level of technology, the intent was totally progressive — to take the best of what the good life of the city had to offer, but to live in the peace of the bush. When I can afford a fax machine and a satellite dish I will receive national and international TV and radio, and be able to talk to anyone, anywhere on the planet. This will be the beginnings of the global village.'

It is necessary to know something of David's life in the bush to understand his work. He sees himself as a colonial Englishman living in an exotic land, for he seldom ventures further from the house in summer than the swimming hole in the creek, preferring to work on the terrace or his small workshop attached to the house. For him (unlike Robert Parker), the bush is an alien space best admired from the house. This cultural isolation within a wilderness leads David to the conviction that there is very little Australian influence in his work, looking instead to Europe for his reading, philosophy and inspiration. This is difficult to reconcile as you view the

**Proteus chairs, banksia and beefwood.**
Photographer: David Tucker.

Sydney blue gum log which lies fallen at the edge of his terrace, already marked with the lines for his next set of wood sculptures, or his Proteus chairs with their sculptured insect forms. As the blowflies buzz around our head, gentle mountain drizzle drips from the roof and the grey green light of the gully fills the room, one wonders what David's work would have been like if he had returned to the border hills of Wales with its man-made landscape.

He contends that Australia is a polyglot of cultural influences, none of which seems dominant. 'Recently my wife Llyn was modelling for me in the courtyard. She was reading Shakespeare while lying on a Balinese sarong, under a Japanese maple next to a creek, under an Australian sky. This typifies for me the cultural mix which is Australia. I hope that the chair I've designed for this book reflects my lifestyle and explains how I feel about living here. A mix of Bauhaus and Delacroix's *Harem* — an exotic simplicity.'

*The Moon Rising* **chair,
Australian red cedar and
blackwood.**
Photographer: David
Tucker.

Simplicity is the hallmark of David Tucker's furniture. Perhaps something of those fundamentalist philosophies of the early settlement are retained, expressed as an examination of function or intent at the beginning of any design. Most craftsmen who are to make a chair begin with sketches or an idea translated into prototype. Few begin with a written review of its function which is a philosophical statement of need. This is the unusual process undertaken by David for bronze and wood sculpture or furniture, and perhaps is the reason for his furniture often being appraised as if it were sculpture. There is a 'paring to the bone' of all members in a chair and a philosophical refinement about their purpose in the structure, which is distinctive. 'The notes I write when beginning a chair ask the question *"why?"* continually, to challenge those preconceptions which can get translated into drawings without you appreciating how the thought was developed.'

Both Robert Parker and David Tucker acknowledge the contribution of each other to their work. They worked together for two years, sharing a workshop, until they began to move in different directions. Robert established Cockatoo Creek Timbers and was involved more with milling and seasoning timber, while David began sculpting. He reflects, 'In the early days, when we were working with sculptured shapes in furniture, we'd literally pass the part-completed components of a chair to each other and let the other person continue without comment. It was a very good time of learning and experimenting. It's wonderful to have someone to bounce ideas off who is constantly appraising your work. As I learnt more about trees and their structure, I was drawn back to my continuing love of sculpture. It was as if I'd passed through a phase in life and was moving on. I'll continue to make furniture, but it will be part of my sculpture work.'

David has always drawn, when designing or as personal experience and interest, but recently he was asked by a gallery to show some of his drawings at an exhibition of his sculpture. He agreed, and was surprised to find that all the drawings sold on the opening night. He is now working harder at his drawings and incorporating them into his work and exhibitions. They are simple expressive line drawings with the same economy of purpose shown in his other work.

His furniture is sold through a few gallery outlets, and the pieces are collector's items for a small clientele. He acknowledges the part played by the NSW Woodworkers Group in promoting his work. 'I exhibited in their first show in the Sydney Opera House and was asked to write a page about myself for the catalogue. I found it difficult, so I wrote, "I like making things. I delight in stimulating transport." This was both too cryptic and short for them, and I was asked to be more serious. But that sums up nicely my reason for working in wood. I enjoy the process of making, and I enjoy those moments of transportation when you look at something or hear something and are moved to stop in wonder.'

There are many things in David Tucker's daily life which must give him that 'transport of delight'. One has only to look through the window at that gully and listen.

*Dance to the Moon*, blue gum.
Photographer: David Tucker.

*Woman Looking Up*, Australian red cedar.
Photographer: David Tucker.

*Saltim Banque*, blue gum.
Photographer: David Tucker.

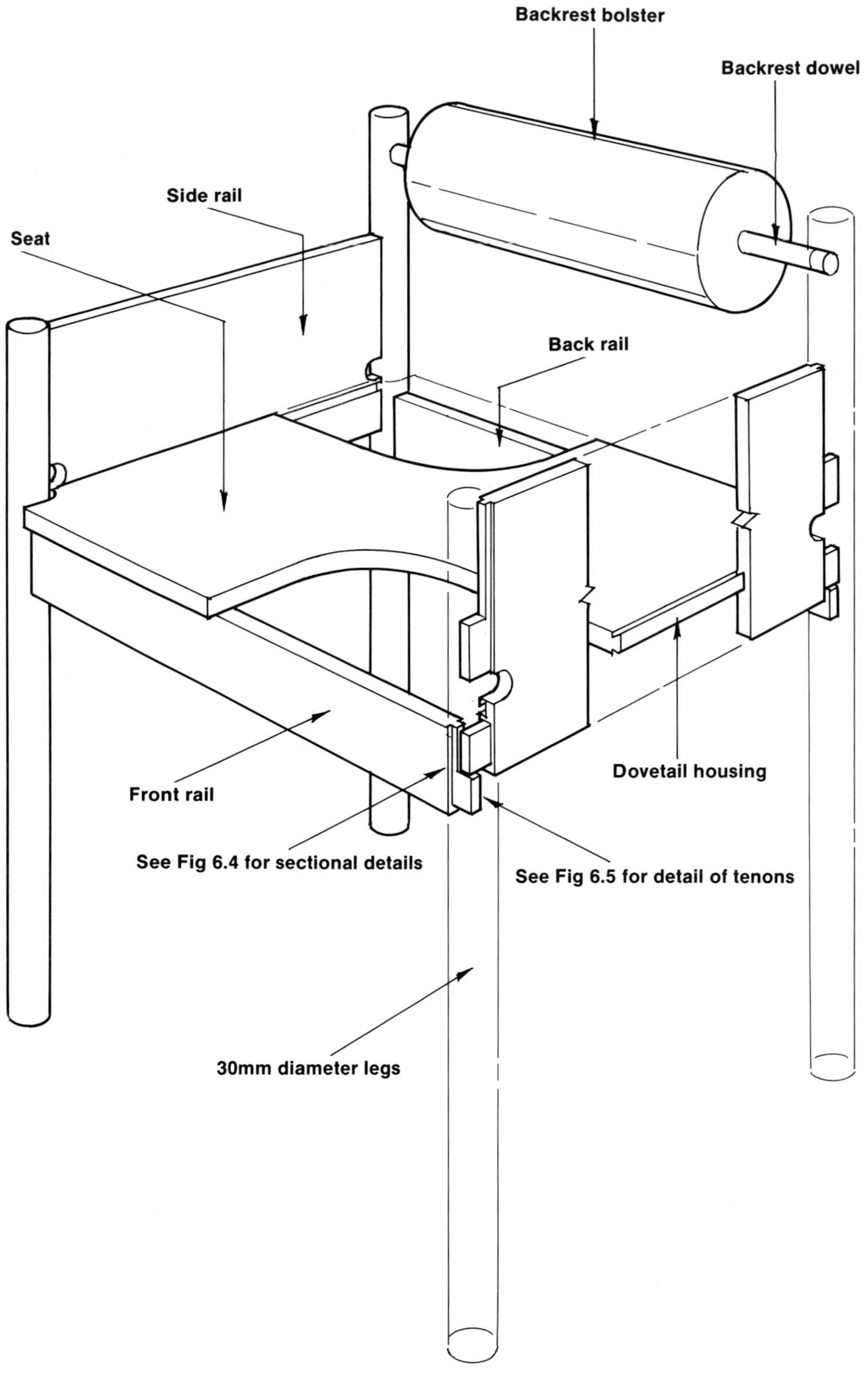

**Fig 6.2 Anatomy of the Valencia chair.**

**Backrest bolster**

**Backrest dowel**

**Side rail**

**Seat**

**Back rail**

**Dovetail housing**

**Front rail**

**See Fig 6.4 for sectional details**

**See Fig 6.5 for detail of tenons**

**30mm diameter legs**

The final design for his chair satisfied the brief. With a seat cushion 20mm thick, the seat height of David's chair is 460mm. This height is 'normal' for chairs used for upright sitting, such as when writing or general office use. If you make a chair for your personal use with a flat, horizontal seat, it is critical for your comfort that you determine what height suits your physique and scale the design accordingly.

David has made the front and back rails and legs from rose she-oak, commonly known as forest oak. It is a dense, hard and straight-grained timber, and provides the strength required of slender legs and finely sectioned members in a chair. It also has highly decorative medullary ray patterns when quarter-sawn. The seat and side rails are made from coachwood, which is light and tough with a cream colour and close grain. The contrast in colour and texture of these two timbers adds a great deal to the final effect. Timber selection is an important element in the total design.

# Making the chair

In most chairs it is possible to identify legs, rails and a seat as the basic elements. Designs vary most in the proportions of these members, and their position in the structure for each member has a similar function in different designs.

In David Tucker's chair, the seat and side rails form three sides of an open box-like structure and are jointed with dovetailed housings. Because dimensions of this open box determine the final size of other members and joints, it should be made first. Haunched mortice and tenon joints are used between the legs and the rails and are shaped to avoid having intersecting mortices in legs and to allow for the 18mm diameter, semi-circular tape holes in the side rails. If you decide to vary these joints, be careful to consider these factors.

## Making the seat and side rail assembly

- As the timber for the seat is 445mm wide, it will have to be jointed from a number of boards. The width of each board is not critical, but to reduce cupping each board should not exceed 150mm wide. Thickness the boards to 17mm and cut to lengths of 460mm. Plane the edges to form gap-free edge joints and glue to form a panel. Plane the panel to a final thickness of 15mm, then dress to a width of 445mm and cut to a length of 530mm.

- Prepare the two side rails to sectional size 190mm x 15mm and cut to a length of 445mm.

- Mark the location of the dovetail joint on the end of the seat and the inside face of the side rails. The underside of the seat is 36mm from the bottom edge of the side rail, as shown in Fig 6.3. This joint is best formed with a dovetail bit in a router, but can be cut with tenon saw and chisel. Shape the four corners of the seat to provide a 2mm clearance from the legs, as shown in Fig 6.4.

- Set out the tenons on the side rails as shown in Fig 6.5. Bore the

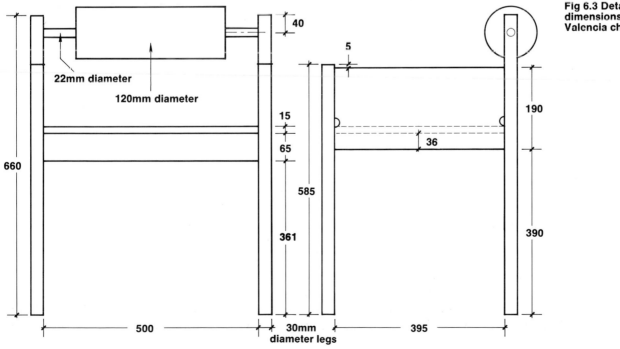

**Fig 6.3 Detailed dimensions of the Valencia chair.**

**Fig 6.4 Top view of the front left-hand or back right-hand legs.**

**Fig 6.5 Detailed dimensions for the tenons on the front, back and side rails.**

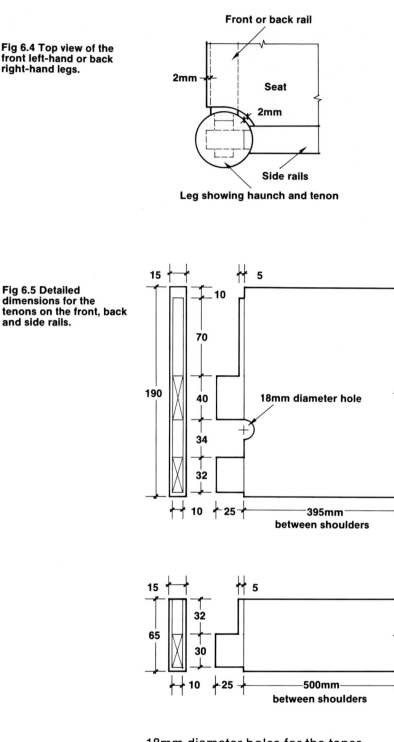

Front or back rail

2mm

Seat

2mm

Side rails

Leg showing haunch and tenon

15

5

10

70

190

40

18mm diameter hole

34

32

10   25   395mm
between shoulders

15

5

32

65

30

10   25   500mm
between shoulders

18mm diameter holes for the tapes before cutting the tenons.

## Making the legs

• Prepare the legs to sectional size 35mm x 35mm and cut the front and back legs to lengths of 615mm and 730mm respectively. (Note that 15mm waste has been allowed on either end of each leg.)

• The mortices can be set out and chopped while the timber is square or after the timber is turned to the finished diameter of 30mm. The setting out for the mortices and the 20mm diameter backrest dowel shown in Fig 6.6 applies only if the mortices are to be chopped before turning. This allows for easier morticing, as the timber can be held securely and the mortices cut square with the edges and faces of the timber. However, greater care is needed when turning, as the mortices provide planes of weakness in the timber and the woodturning gouge and chisel can dig into the mortice edge if heavy cuts are made. To reduce 'whipping' when turning such thin legs, a lathe steady should be used. Fig 6.7 shows a simple steady which can be made from scrap timber. Fine sand each leg before removing from the lathe.

• If the legs are turned to 30mm diameter before marking out and chopping the tenons, the position of the mortices can be marked while each leg is in the lathe. The measurements shown in Fig 6.6 can be marked on the surface of the legs approximately 90° apart and the mortices chopped with the leg held securely in a vice or V-block. Care should be taken to ensure that the mortice chisel or bit is at 90° to the previous cut.

## Making the front and back rails

• Prepare the rails to sectional size 65mm x 15mm and cut to a length of 540mm.

• Assemble the seat and side rails, then the front and back legs to the side rails, and cramp the joints lightly. On the front and back rails, mark the length between shoulders for the tenons, marking off from the inside face of the legs. This measurement could vary slightly from the 500mm shown in Fig 6.3. Complete the setting out of the tenons as shown in Fig 6.5 and cut

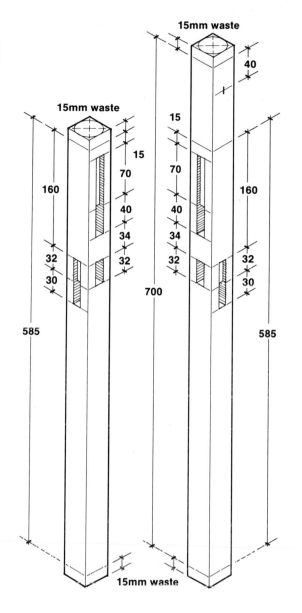

15mm waste

15mm waste

40

15

15

70

70

160

40

40

160

34

34

32

32

32

32

30

30

160

700

585

585

15mm waste

will allow for expansion and contraction of the seat panel.

● Fine sand, apply four coats of fine furniture wax and buff to a finish.

## Making the backrest bolster

● The cover for the bolster is made from Ikat fabric, but any firm upholstery fabric would be suitable.

● Glue dense foam 12mm thick by one edge to the dowel. When dry, the foam is wrapped tightly around the dowel to form a 120mm diameter cylinder and taped to hold it in a roll.

● Feed 20mm wide black tape through edge loops in the Ikat cover and wrap the cover around the roll with an end flap tucked in. The cover is tensioned by lacing fitted through eyelets along both ends of the cover. The lacing is pulled tight and tied around the dowel. The 20mm black side tapes are pulled tight and the ends tied in a bow around the dowel.

**Fig 6.6 Setting out for mortices on the front and back legs.**

the tenons.

● Turn the backrest dowel to 20mm diameter using a lathe steady similar to that shown in Fig 6.7, and finish to a length of 550mm.

## Assembly and finishing

● Sand all members to a fine finish.

● Glue the legs to the front and back rails to form a front and back assembly and cramp lightly, checking that the rails are square to the legs. Leave until the glue is completely dry.

● The seat is fitted to the side rails. **Do not glue the dovetail joints.** This

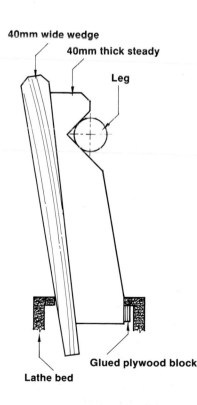

40mm wide wedge

40mm thick steady

Leg

Lathe bed

Glued plywood block

**Fig 6.7 Simple lathe steady used to turn 30mm diameter legs.**

61

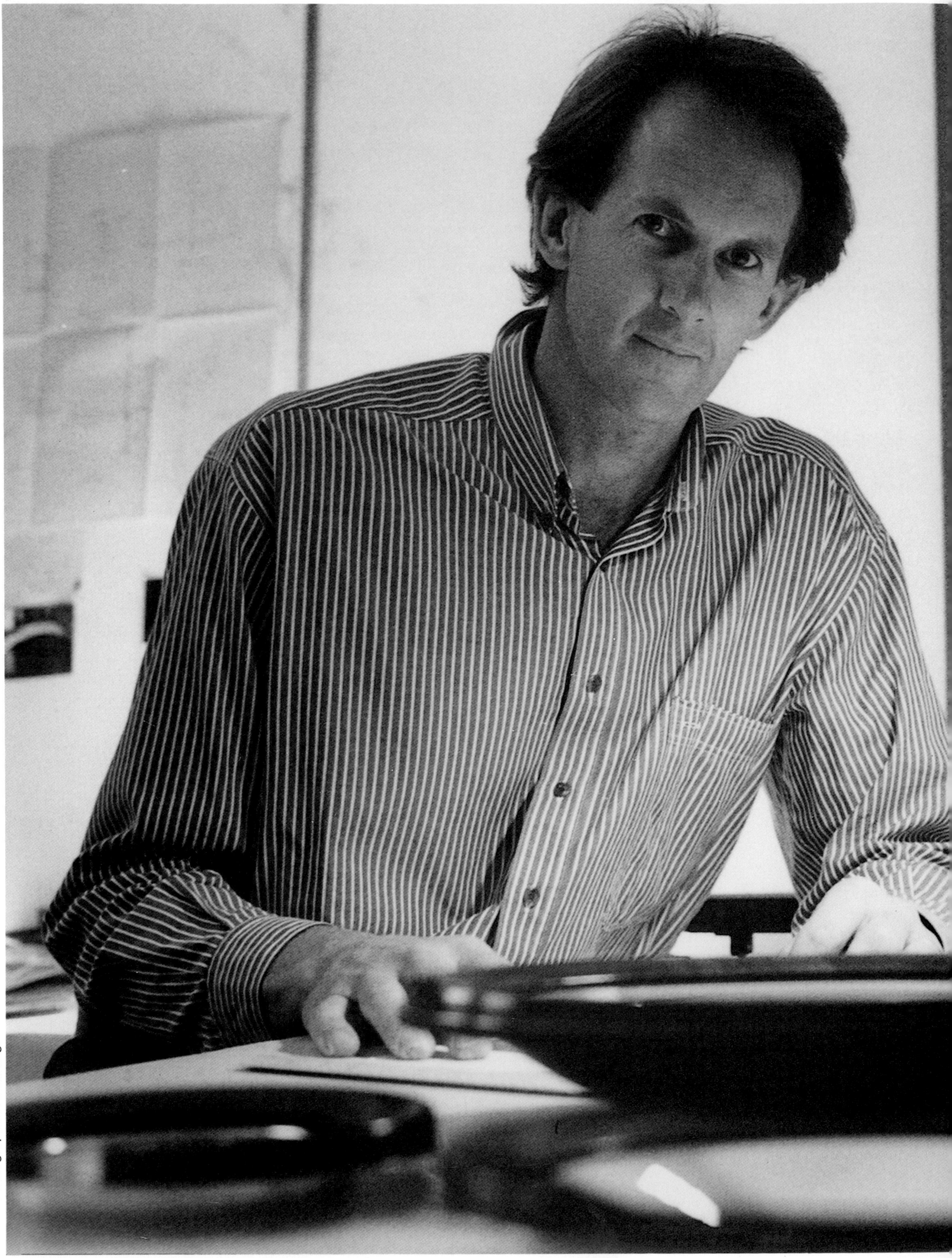

Photographer: A. Lelong.

Most woodworkers do not have an office. It might be an area of their showroom or merely a bundle of papers thrown under the coffee table at home. All have a different approach to the organisation of their work. Leslie John Wright is a designer-maker whose preference for an office is a designer's studio. The desk at which he sits is large and of sycamore, steel and glass, stylish but functional. The filing cabinet at his back with its blond timber, minute handles and immaculate proportions complements the modern drafting machine against the mantlepiece. His clothes are in muted tones and fashionably casual. Everything displays a thoughtfulness for presentation which explains much about the man and his work. Here the baggy clothes, work boots and dust-laden countenance of the average woodworker are out of place, for Leslie presents himself faithfully in speech and manner as a polished professional. I wonder if it has always been so; perhaps even when he was farming, near Denmark on the south coast of Western Australia in the 1970s, the landscape would have been well formed and the function of that farm part of an equally structured plan.

His current studio is in a Victorian house on the outskirts of Fremantle facing the Canning Highway, the road to Perth. The Swan River is across the highway and the Fremantle docks around the bend beyond a bridge. A workshop fills the rear of the house, as precise and functional as the office. A small plaque on the gate says 'Leslie John Wright — Designer.'

I was surprised to learn that Leslie, like Greg Collins and Robert Parker, is an ardent surfer. Many of his contemporaries from those idyllic days surfing on the south coast, who shared waves and sunsets, are now working as creative professionals. It either says something about those who sought the alternative lifestyle of the 1970s, or the quality of that experience in throwing people back on to 'the nature of their soul'. He still surfs each morning at Cottesloe Beach, but misses the better waves of the south. He says, 'To me the sea is very important. Surfing is a way of relating to nature which is unique. Perhaps it's the time of contemplation I enjoy between sets, certainly there's a great energy release in the surf. It's a wonderful source of inspiration for me.' It is significant that his first success as a designer, the Shoreline deck chair, made from laminated timber, is shown in promotional material sitting in the wash of a wave on a beach. Leslie, Greg and Robert all talk of the surf with much the same passion as Gay Hawkes or Kevin Perkins talk of south-west Tasmania, or Michael Gill about the trees at Plum Pudding Brush, or David Tucker of Mozart. We are all 'transported' as individuals by those things we can relate to directly. My problem is with a mental image of Leslie John Wright, hair dishevelled, barefooted, board under arm, leg rope dangling, walking from the surf. To me it has very little in common with his studio, the professional image and the classical lines of the furniture he creates. It will ever remain a mystery, but he assures me he will always have a preference for the informalities of board shorts and beach to coat and tie. This casualness is an expression of the Australian lifestyle from which he draws much of his creativity.

**Shoreline deck chairs, laminated Huon pine.**
Photographer: Leslie John Wright.

Leslie refers to his 10 years in the country as an experience as sculptor on a grand scale, where he was able to shape a landscape and think about qualities of form and texture and our relationship with the environment. He left for a grand tour of Europe with his family in 1981, and the discoveries he made spurred him to further his creative longings. Returning,

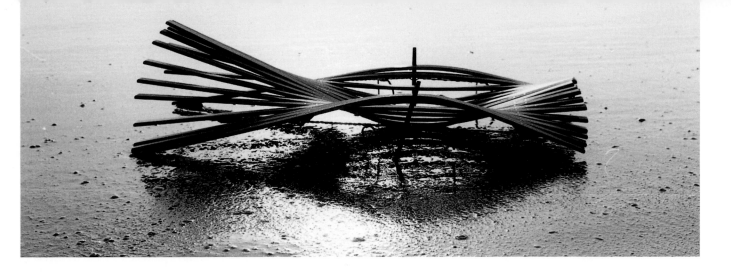

**Tensioned Form**, 1983, beech and copper fittings.
Photographer: Leslie John Wright.

he enrolled in a degree course in design at Perth's Curtin University. 'Once a friend asked me at that time how long I had been studying design and I said, "About 31 years", because I recognised that I'd always looked at everything I saw and used critically. I'd always been better at art than other subjects at school, but ignored my potential until well into my twenties. In the latter years in Denmark I took up photography, drawing and watercolours. I had some early success at photography, and won a number of awards. When I entered the design course at Curtin University, I could have gone in a number of directions. Originally I thought of specialising in photography and graphics, but soon realised that these activities were too transient for my liking. In the first year we had the opportunity to work in different mediums, and I found myself gravitating to the workshops, where ultimately I majored in furniture design and minored in jewellery. I suppose that explains why I embellish most of my furniture with semi-precious materials. I delight in relating other materials to wood.'

The transition to a practice as designer was difficult. He says, 'In retrospect I was very naive starting off by myself. It would have been better to work with an architect or designer for a few years before establishing my own studio. Greg Collins and I were strongly influenced by Michael Cooper, the Californian wood sculptor, who visited Western Australia. We made a close study of his approach, which pretty much damned the conventions of cabinetmaking. He was a master craftsman who rarely used anything like wood chisels, which was a great discovery for me because I'm not particularly disciplined with hand tools. I don't consider myself a cabinetmaker or woodworker for that matter. I guess as a designer I conceptualise a form and, like Michael Cooper, find a way of creating that form. It would rarely involve dovetail joints, and I don't believe in the 1990s we should ever need to think of such a process. Conventional expectations in furniture construction are hard to break down. If I had come from a cabinetmaking background, I might never have resolved some of the forms I have been able to develop.'

He was amazed at the response to his first products, elevated turned bowls which sold to Sydney corporations for prices which were realistic but nonetheless expensive. This experience, he now reflects, gave him a false sense of confidence which led him to believe that he could take on anything. His first commission as a designer was for light fittings in steel and fabric, and with it came the realisation of the difficulties he faced when working with unfamiliar materials and the problems inherent in prototyping.

In 1985 Leslie left on a five-month overseas trip to visit workshops and colleges which taught design. He talked to artists and designer-makers in such places as the Wendell Castle Workshop in the USA, the Royal Academy of Art in Copenhagen and the School for Craftsmen in Wood in England, but it was the experience of Italy which eclipsed everything he had experienced on the tour. He relates, 'I spent the last five weeks in Italy, where art seems to be an inherent way of life in society and where industry holds designers in high regard. It's obvious that Italian designers have a good relationship with the artisans who make what they design. I returned with enormous enthusiasm to be a multi-medium designer like those I had seen in Italy, but soon realised that the lack of comparable infrastructure wouldn't support my aspirations. I set up my workshop to work mostly in wood with the help of a fellowship from the West Australian Department for the Arts, and entered a number of exhibitions. I worked across a range of disciplines from photography to graphics and woodturning, but soon realised the need to specialise. I felt overwhelmed. There was just too much to learn. At that stage I didn't even know what a job sheet was! When my workshop was set up, I learnt the wood processes I needed to know as I encountered the next problem in making each piece. I've never really been taught joint construction and my skills were limited, but if I had known more I probably wouldn't have designed the way I design. However, I need the workshop facility and I doubt that I'll ever create anything significant directly off the drawing board without going through the processes of modelling, prototyping and redesigning.

'It has taken me years to learn how to cost jobs, and it remains a major difficulty as I'm continually working with unknowns in construction details. Several years ago I was asked to design and make a set of chairs and a table for the Victoria Ministry of Arts, which was a great honour. It was a very complex design, and we consulted by fax. The Crest chairs were laminated, and I experimented with many different glue types in making the prototype. In retrospect, it would have been near-impossible to estimate the labour involved in that commission. It's a constant problem working on the edge of understanding. I now see it as risky business practice to expect to carry the cost of discovery in developing innovative works.'

While he would like to work on individual commissions and exhibitions, he also recognises the need for a number of small production designs which can be sold through galleries or bought as corporate gifts. At the time of our discussion a set of boxed silk scarves sat on his drawing board ready for delivery. The work was commissioned. Like a number of other materials and processes, fabric design appeals to him and the scarves, or small products like them, could provide a much-needed cash flow. Next to the scarves were a set of spun silver dishes with turned wooden rims, which could satisfy the same need.

The cost of displaying work in exhibitions is proving prohibitive. 'I recently completed a pavilion console table for exhibition at a gallery in the coastal town of Yallingup. The table was expensive to make, there were subcontractors involved who had to be paid, and it cost me two days out of my studio and $400 to get it there. It's not something you would want to repeat often. That table is one of three to be made, with near-identical bases but with different tops. The table in the gallery has a top made from Tasmanian myrtle burl veneer, while the others are to be glass and polished black marble. I suppose this form of promotion has to be costed out as part of

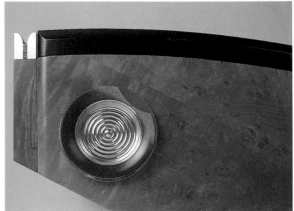

**Detail of Pavilion console table, Tasmanian myrtle with silver fittings and stone inlay. Atoll bowl in silver and native pear.**
Photographer: A. Lelong.

**Pavilion console table, jarrah with patinated bronze fittings.**
Photographer: R. Garvey.

# Gymnos Dining Table

**Gymnos table, sycamore, aluminium and leather.**
© **Leslie John Wright.**
Photographer: Robert Garvey.

**G**ymnos is an eight-seater dining table which represents a return by Leslie John Wright to the figurative form as a source for ideas after a number of planar architectural designs. When designing any piece of furniture, the characteristics of the material being used, its strength, directional stability and rigidity are paramount in determining the final form of the piece. Timber has some 'unlikable' characteristics such as splitting along the grain and movement caused by changes in atmospheric conditions. We overcome these deficiencies by making allowance for them when designing. Legs on tables are a good example of this. The load on a table leg is longitudinal as the leg is usually vertical. This should allow legs of very slender dimensions to be used, but look at the legs on conventional tables — they are usually robust, if not heavy. The reason for this is to allow for jointing of rails to the leg or to give the table lateral stability without

bracing. To feel a table sway sideways when you lean against it is hardly a comforting sensation.

Naming a component of a table as a 'leg' recognises that, like us, it must stand on something. The use of anatomically inspired legs is not new in either period or contemporary furniture. The problem with this form of leg, however, is that timber as a structural material is not bone, and we lack the ability to recreate the joint and cartilage which enables our own legs and those of four-legged animals to assume poses where the components are at acute angles. When designing an anatomically inspired table leg, these problems are overcome usually by subtly *suggesting* a knee, as in a cabriole leg, while allowing any load to be transmitted vertically through the leg. In some French period furniture the 'knee' was distinctly angled, but the problem created by short grain around the knee was overcome by making the leg massive in section with internal rails to distribute the load.

Leslie John Wright's Gymnos table uses aluminium in that portion of the table where timber would not have sufficient strength. This limited use of an alternative material has liberated the design. As Leslie says, 'Working with the energies evoked by the gymnast has created new directions for expressive forms. Here the making of furniture which is naturally of human scale can, through the physical act of carving and forming, become an extension of body action. The performance of the ballet dancer, gymnast and archer inspired my early concepts. It's as if this table was formed by stretching fabric between

**Detail of the leg of Gymnos table.**
Photographer: Robert Garvey.

diagonally opposed forces. These forces, like sinews, connect the legs to the table top, and are made from cast aluminium with the legs carved from sycamore.'

## Making the table

There are many unusual features in the design of this table to satisfy woodworkers seeking a challenge. The table employs a number of unique concepts in construction, but they all use skills little different from those used for centuries. The body of the table was drawn using computer-assisted drafting techniques, and the profiles of the many ribs made from 7mm marine ply which form the 'honeycomb' of the body, were cut using a computer-directed router. Boat builders have used hand and eye for generations to produce similar complex curves without difficulty. Those boat-building principles can be used to generate a comparable curve on the underside of the Gymnos table.

**Detail of the leather underside of the Gymnos table.**
Photographer: Robert Garvey.

The irregular table top is shaped like a shallow bowl with a leg at each corner. Sycamore veneer is used for the table top, with the perimeter frame made from the same timber. The curved underside is formed by a leather membrane, tensioned drum-like over the ribs of the table. The aluminium sections of the legs penetrate the surface of the table top to define their position in the table and to give an adequate bearing surface between the leg and the table top. A square tenon on the sculptured sycamore leg fits into a mortice in the aluminium casting. The leg is bonded to the casting using an epoxy glue, while the same glue, with bolts and machine screws, holds the casting to the body of the table top.

### Making the table top

• Draw the full-size shape of the table top on to a flat surface. Mark the location of each leg with the perimeter frame also marked, as shown in the plan view in Fig 7.1.

• Cut the ribs to shape from 7mm marine ply. If not computer-developed, the shapes can be determined by drawing progressive true shapes of sections of the body of the table top. Each rib is cut slightly oversize to allow for final shaping. Once jointed and assembled, the rib structure is screwed and glued to a 12mm sycamore veneered MDF board cut to the shape of the table top (minus the perimeter frame). Trim the outer edges of the ribs to fit the shape of the table profile.

• Shape and profile from sycamore the four sections which form the perimeter frame. Fit these to butt neatly against the edge of the veneered MDF board and the ribs. Glue the perimeter frame to the table top and ribs.

• Using a thin batten bent across the ribs as a guide, dress the edges of the ribs to give a consistent curve on the underside of the table.

### Making the legs

• Carve the wooden patterns for

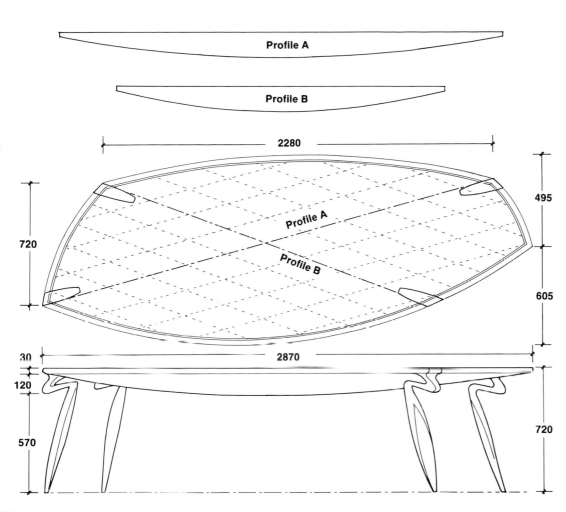

Profile A

Profile B

2280

720

495

605

Profile A

Profile B

30

2870

120

570

720

Fig 7.1 Dimensions of Gymnos table showing the ribs forming the table top.

the aluminium castings. Note that the cast section of the leg is in two parts which are later joined. Each cast section of the leg is identical, but the positioning of the leg will require the aluminium casting to be shaped to fit the profile of the table. Have a qualified person cast the leg to ensure that all the castings are sound.

• Shape the top section of each casting to fit the profile of the table at each location, polish the castings and anodise. Mark out the recess necessary to accommodate the casting on the table top and remove the timber and fit each casting to a gap-free joint flush with the surface of the table. Fit the tightening bolts and machine screws securing the casting to the body of the table top, as shown in Fig 7.2.

• Fit the bottom half of the casting to the top half and bond permanently with the aid of a pivot/screw connector.

• Carve the sycamore lower leg to shape. A tenon on the leg fits into a hole in the casting and is bonded to the casting with a epoxy.

• Dress off all surfaces on the legs flush to give continuous flowing lines.

73

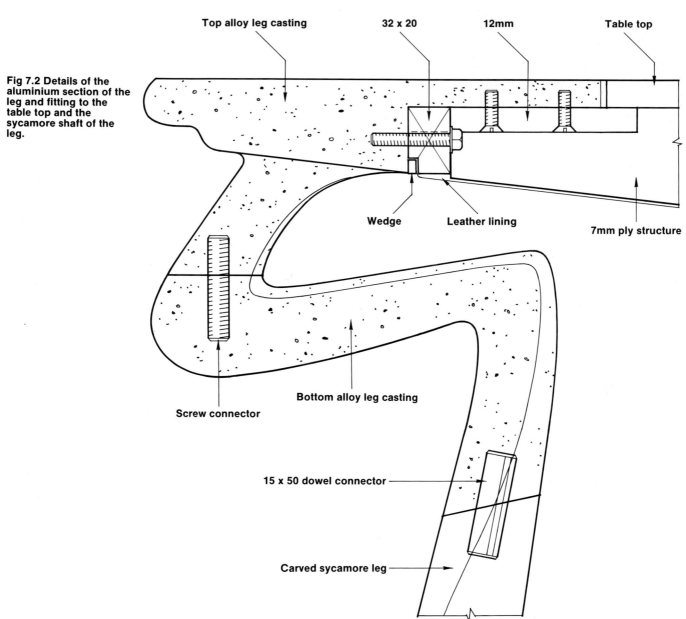

Fig 7.2 Details of the aluminium section of the leg and fitting to the table top and the sycamore shaft of the leg.

Top alloy leg casting

32 x 20

12mm

Table top

Wedge

Leather lining

7mm ply structure

Screw connector

Bottom alloy leg casting

15 x 50 dowel connector

Carved sycamore leg

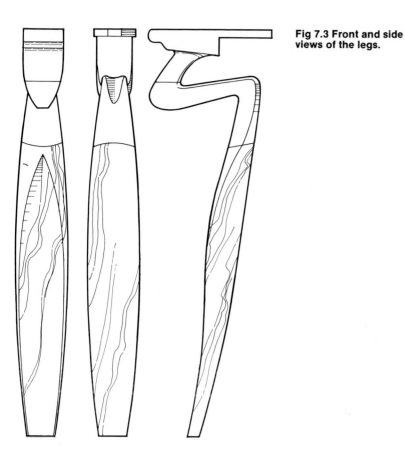

Fig 7.3 Front and side views of the legs.

## Finishing and assembly

• Cut an 8mm x 5mm groove on the inside under edge of the perimeter frame to provide a recess for securing the edge of the leather membrane.

• Clean up and sand all surfaces to a final finish.

• Fix the legs to the table top using an epoxy glue with securing bolts and screws.

• Spray finish with a satin finish polyurethane.

• Cut the leather membrane in segments and stitch the segments to provide a continuous cover. Stretch the membrane over the ribs. Secure the outer edge of the membrane in the 8mm x 5mm groove, trim and fix firmly with a closing batten.

*Grant Vaughan*

Grant Vaughan had wanted to apply another coat of Danish oil to a cedar table, so we moved from the verandah to his workshop and continued our discussions as he brushed on the oil. I asked where the cedar planks which were stacked at the door had come from, and he told me the history of 'cedar-getting' on the north coast of New South Wales as if describing a gold strike at Ballarat or the Klondike. Suddenly he remembered the table. The Danish oil had begun to set up, sticky and binding. We rubbed furiously as rain rattled on the workshop roof and sweat dripped from my chin. The surface glowed a spangled ruby red as sprays of refracted light changed in depth and colour as eye followed arm. Australian cedar has always been prized for its rich colour, and Grant's home in Rocky Valley, near Lismore, was in cedar-getting country in the 19th century. Cedar is now 'cut out' and few trees remain, retained as family secrets in remote gullies or hoarded as planks to be sold when the price is right. Grant Vaughan is careful in his dealings with cedar-getters, as at $4000 per cubic metre it is a questionable trade in the valley.

We sat on the verandah that morning talking about his sources of inspiration and the problems of selling in a capricious marketplace. Grant Vaughan left university after studying but not completing engineering and architecture degree courses. Born in the country, the prospect of working confined to an office in a city made him uneasy. He returned to the north coast and began making simple furniture for a local store. An uncle left him a legacy, and he purchased an old dairy farm in Rock Valley and established a workshop with a friend. The partnership did not last, as Grant became more serious about designing and investing in the business. Since 1979 he has worked alone, moving the workshop from the cow bale to a timber shed and building a home by degrees. It now sits amongst fruit trees and an ancient Moreton Bay fig on the side of a ridge. Hills rise to the west and a creek flows below the house. A restful place to work and contemplate nature.

Carved bowls have become Grant Vaughan's trademark, as they provided his first success when displayed in galleries and exhibitions in Sydney. They have distinctive rolled edges, a lip

**Carved bowl, Australian red cedar, 300mm diameter.**
Photographer: John McCormick.

being formed from compound curves terminating with a shape resembling a pouring spout. His inspiration came from natural forms, the lip being similar to the rolled edge on the petal of a *Monstera deliciosa* (Swiss cheese plant). The first bowl was modelled in clay, but he now determines the final shape in his mind and carves it without modification. Most bowls are in red cedar, a soft open-pored timber. Those experienced in carving this wood can only marvel at the fineness of those long, thinly formed lips. The line is sweeping, continuous and immaculately finished. It was a natural extension to carve oval mirrors, and these have provided cash in lean times.

Most woodworkers claim that it is difficult to sell from exhibitions, as visitors are interested in looking rather than buying. Grant has had continued success at exhibitions, both with sales and awards. He has won many of the most prestigious awards on the 'woodworkers' circuit' in Australia for both furniture design and carving. When challenged as to the reason for this success, he states with suitable modesty that he has never had difficulty selling his work. I then asked whether he had been successful at assessing the market and restricting his work to that which would sell. He replied, 'I guess I do consider what is saleable and the pricing of a piece. It's doubtful if that really does limit my work. I still make what I enjoy making, and they are my designs, not an adaption of someone else's. I have refused local commissions because it wasn't what I would be happy making. It's probable that discipline in my work has been a good thing and has guided me into simple shapes. By adding 200 hours' labour to a piece of furniture you're not necessarily going to improve either its aesthetics or its function. As well, most of my clients are conservative, so I have that restriction to consider. I have thought recently that I'd like to experiment more, and I've applied for Craft Council grants to give me time to do this, but without success. I've thought of teaching, which would give me contact with others. That would be nice, as I'm getting tired of being a hermit woodworker.'

Some woodworkers who had commissions for the New Parliament House in Canberra had problems of scale and work schedules. Grant had his share of frustrations, although he can now reflect on the experience with satisfaction and an occasional wry smile, as he completed the assignment exhausted. He initially welcomed the open brief he was given to design and make two identical display cabinets for the entry to the Senate Offices. They were to have climatically controlled interiors for the storage and display of precious documents. He began the project in August 1987, and completed it the following May. Red bean was selected from timber purchased by the New Parliament House Construction

Authority, but it proved too hard for the carved surfaces required in the design. He has never added up the hours taken to make the cabinets as he fears the final figure might be too distressing to bear. He summed it up with a shrug of the shoulders: 'I can't honestly say I enjoyed all of it, as having strict deadlines to meet and delays in starting construction created lots of stress. Besides gaining experience working on a major commission, there were other positives. I was given extensive tours of the building, looking at design elements which tie the whole building together. It was interesting gaining an insight into other people's approach and their resolution of design problems.'

Grant found his engineering studies useful in this experience, as he rarely uses workshop drawings in his normal

**Display case, Senate Chamber, New Parliament House, Canberra, Australian red cedar, red bean and brass.**
Photographer: Matt Kelso.

**Table, New Guinea walnut bleached, 1400mm x 620mm x 400mm.**
Photographer: Greg Piper.

work. He admits that most designs evolve in his head and he seldom makes prototypes, relying on thinking the design through in his mind then solving the problems in the final piece as it is worked. Although he has not had formal training in cabinet work or wood machining, he claims never to have been frustrated by lack of skills or to have limited his work to what he currently knew. Each project was a personal learning experience, and mistakes were few as he realised the cost. Perhaps it is not only need which ensures rapid learning. He is constantly aware that mistakes in design judgement and construction will materially affect his family.

Grant Vaughan is known for his professional presentation. His brochures and cards have set a standard in graphics amongst woodworkers in Australia, and he acknowledges the work of his wife Paula in their production and the value of this type of promotion. His bowls are well-known throughout Australia, partly because of a beautifully lit photograph which was printed as a postcard and has been reproduced often in brochures and press releases. This singular presentation has been used as a signature and recognised as such.

His furniture designs evolve slowly as he makes slight modifications to add a further level of refinement to each piece. He is currently producing a number of side tables, mostly in bleached silky oak, where edge treatments and leg profiles change in minute detail to improve the unity of concept. Some have described these tables and his mirrors and bowls as Art Nouveau in style, but Grant disagrees with this assessment. 'I feel my tables have a classical influence, but an initial inspiration was followed by months of sweat and tears. Timbers also influence me. I'm making more bleached furniture of late. Perhaps I'm getting weary of working in red timbers. Pale colours look most effective on larger tables where shadow lines are more noticeable, which helps to define the shape.'

**Carved and turned bowl, camphor laurel bleached, 360mm diameter.** Photographer: Greg Piper.

Later that afternoon we retreated once more to the cool of the verandah and remained until hordes of mosquitoes drove us inside. His soft voice and friendly, disarming manner made conversation easy. It would be difficult to argue with Grant Vaughan; he seems to be at peace with himself and the world. There is also something restful in the design of his furniture. It doesn't confront, it has no pretence, it is just beautifully formed and exquisitely made. It is the expression of a craftsman who knows what he likes to make and what it will look like before timber is chosen or tools prepared. Perhaps it is this personal resolution of the design in his mind which causes it to naturally reflect his own tranquillity. Grant is fortunate that so many clients appreciate that resolution and continue to support him so enthusiastically.

**Carved bowl, 340mm diameter, Powerhouse Museum Collection, Sydney.**

# Side Table

Side table, Queensland
silky oak bleached.
© Grant Vaughan.
Photographer: John
McCormick.

rant Vaughan designed the
first side table in 1987 and,
although satisfied with the
proportions, has since
modified the detailing. This
table is made from North Queensland silky
oak, which, although an attractive golden
brown colour, is bleached to provide the
lightness he sought. Quarter-sawn boards in
silky oak have large medullary rays which
appear as dark-coloured flecks. When
finished as a non-reflective surface and lit
with a side light, these flecks appear to float
on a three-dimensional background. In the
initial design, Grant used rounded forms on
all details. With this new design, many
adjacent concave and convex faces join at
sharp edges, yet the flowing lines and

softness are retained. He now aligns the direction of medullary rays in adjoining pieces, which exploits the rich variety of grain patterns and texture of silky oak and gives the impression that the pedestals were carved from solid timber.

Grant Vaughan admits that the original design was inspired by a table carved in stone, which he saw in a film. The pedestals have evolved to their final form and, although visually simple, are complex to make. There are few flat surfaces, and the sharp edges are straight but end in curves. Great care must be taken in selecting the timber to ensure grain patterns match on adjoining members of the pedestal so that joins are not visible.

Blackwood is used as a deep-set insert down the outer edge of each pedestal and as a border to the veneer on the table top. The 9mm x 4mm border on the table top provides a contrasting line separating the quarter-sawn pattern of the silky oak veneer and the backsawn pattern of the solid silky oak edges. When bleached, the fine fiddleback grain of blackwood provides a subtle contrast in texture to silky oak, but is little different in colour.

The table top was veneered with two 3mm thick book-matched sheets which were cut with a bandsaw from a quarter-sawn silky oak board. The veneers were glued with epoxy resin to ensure a waterproof glue line and provide an

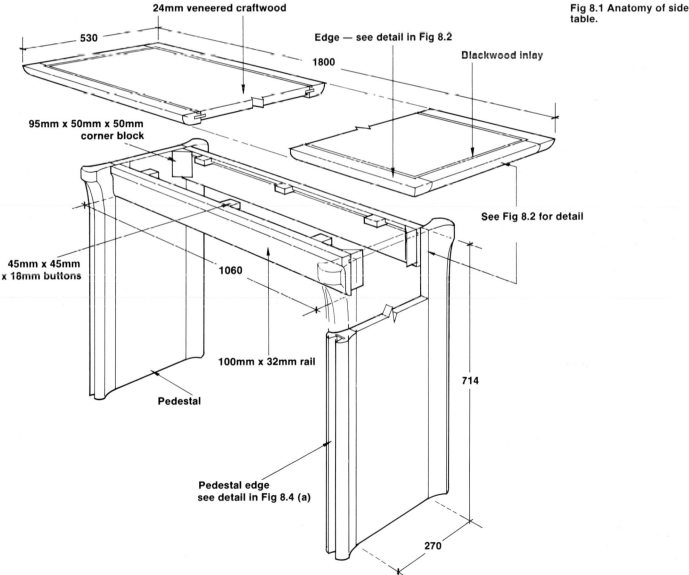

Fig 8.1 Anatomy of side table.

24mm veneered craftwood

530

Edge — see detail in Fig 8.2

1800

Blackwood inlay

95mm x 50mm x 50mm corner block

See Fig 8.2 for detail

45mm x 45mm x 18mm buttons

1060

100mm x 32mm rail

714

Pedestal

Pedestal edge see detail in Fig 8.4 (a)

270

impenetrable seal for the MDF core. All other members were glued with PVA. Each pedestal is made from a solid silky oak board 34mm thick with 100mm x 64mm sections glued to either edge. These edges are made from two laminated boards to simplify shaping and to allow the blackwood inset to be fitted.

Grant Vaughan found it easier to solve the many design and construction problems in this table with simple sketches and by making full-scale models of pedestal details. He admits that he finds it very difficult to obtain 'a good three-dimensional feeling for complex curved surfaces from drawings alone'.

# Making the table

There are five components to the table: a top, two identical pedestals and front and back rails. In this project timber selection is very important to ensure that grain patterns match. It is preferable for the boards to be cut consecutively from the one flitch. If this is not possible, ensure that the colour and grain pattern of adjoining components match, as each pedestal should appear to have been shaped from a solid piece of

timber. If working with rough-sawn boards, it will be necessary to dress one face before deciding how the individual members will be cut from each board.

## Making the top

● Cut the 18mm craftwood core to size and plane or machine trim the edges straight and square to the finished size, 1722mm x 406mm.

● If you use pre-cut veneers for the table top, ensure that they are consecutive layers in a bundle and when unfolded like pages in a book, that the grain pattern is symmetrical about the 'fold'.

● To cut veneers from a plank, dress a face of the board (approximately 1750mm x 210mm) selected for the book match veneers and cut a 4mm thick veneer from the dressed face using a bandsaw. Re-dress the cut face on the board and cut an additional veneer as before. Sand or thickness these veneers to 3mm and trim the fold edge to form a perfect joint line. These two veneers should match along their fold lines. Four

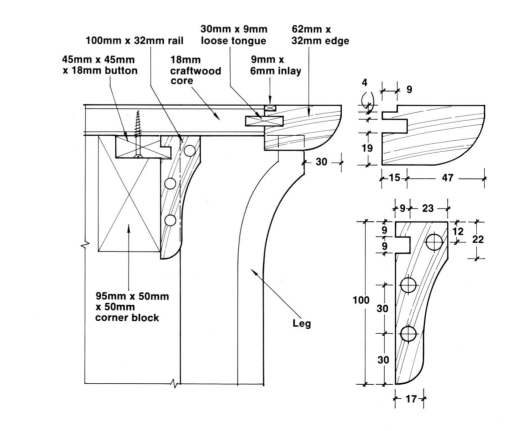

**Fig 8.2 Details of table top and rail.**

such veneers are required, as both faces of the table top are veneered.

• Tape the joins in each matched set of veneers and glue to the craftwood core using epoxy resin glue. Uniform pressure must be applied while the glue dries. Caul boards, bearers and G-cramps, or a vacuum press can be used to apply this pressure.

• When the glue has dried, trim the veneer overlap from the sides, being careful not to undercut the edge.

• Prepare the backsawn timber edges to sectional size, the long edges 62mm x 36mm and the edges for the ends 39mm x 36mm (prepare in multiple lengths allowing approximately 100mm waste for the total length). Commence the shaping shown in Fig 8.2 by rounding over the under edge using a 30mm round over bit in a router or a spindle moulder. Complete the shaping by forming the groove for the 30mm x 9mm plywood loose tongue on the inner edge using a router and slotting cutter bit or a spindle moulder. With the same setting on the machine, form an identical groove in the edge of the veneered core for the 30mm x 9mm plywood loose tongue.

• Cut the timber edges to length. The 39mm x 36mm strips for the ends must be cut accurately to match the width of the veneered core. Cut the 62mm x 36mm edges to 1810mm long, which will allow 5mm waste on each end to be trimmed after the edges are glued to the veneered core.

• Match the joins between the edges and the veneered core to ensure that when cramped they form a gap-free joint.

• Cut the 30mm x 9mm plywood loose tongue to sectional size and cut into suitable lengths. Glue the loose tongue into grooves in the edge of the veneered core, then glue the timber edges on to the tongue. Cramp lightly with sash cramps or straps.

• Dress off waste on the ends and clean up the face using a cabinet scraper, and fine sand the faces.

## Making the pedestals

• Prepare the core for each pedestal to sectional size 270mm x 34mm. If it is not possible to cut each from a single board to achieve the width of 270mm, two or more boards will have to be edge-jointed to give this width. Cut the cores to a length of 714mm.

• Prepare the eight members which will form the pedestal edges to sectional size 100mm x 34mm and cut each to a length of 714mm.

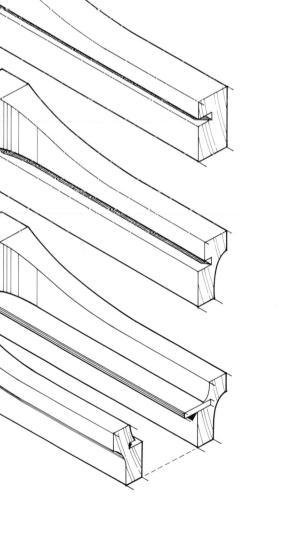

**Fig 8.3 Shaping pedestal edge.**

Cut the grooves to receive the 34mm x 6mm loose tongue in each member, as shown in Fig 8.4 (b).

• Remembering that the edges are formed by four mirror matched pairs, shape the edge members as shown in Fig 8.3. The sectional shape at A, B and C is shown in Fig 8.4 (c). Although a spindle moulder is the ideal machine for this shaping, a router fitted with a core box bit and a slotting cutter could be used. It is necessary to widen out the hollow on the top end by hand with a gouge to give the shape shown in Fig 8.4 (a). When shaping is completed, place the edges together in matched pairs to ensure that the profile formed by this gouge work is symmetrical.

• Prepare the four blackwood loose tongues to sectional size 34mm x 6mm and cut to a length of 714mm.

• Sand the internal faces of each edge member, as this will be difficult once they are glued together. Assemble the edges by gluing the blackwood spline into the grooves on each pair and cramp lightly until the glue dries.

• Dress the inside face of each pedestal edge and match it to an edge on the pedestal core to ensure that a gap-free glue line can be achieved. Assemble the pedestals by gluing each pedestal edge to the pedestal core, cramping lightly until the glue has dried. Dress the glue lines to give a continuous flowing surface between the pedestal edges and the core.

• Prepare the two rails to sectional size 100mm x 32mm and cut each to a length of 1060mm. Shape to the section shown in Fig 8.2. Mark the centres for the three dowels on the end of each rail and transfer these marks to the matching position on the pedestals. Drill holes for 100mm x 12mm diameter dowels.

• Prepare four corner blocks and six timber buttons as detailed in Fig 8.2.

Fig 8.4 (a) Side and end view of pedestal.
(b) Laminated silky oak and blackwood tongue for pedestal edge before shaping.
(c) Sectional shapes of pedestal edge at A, B and C.

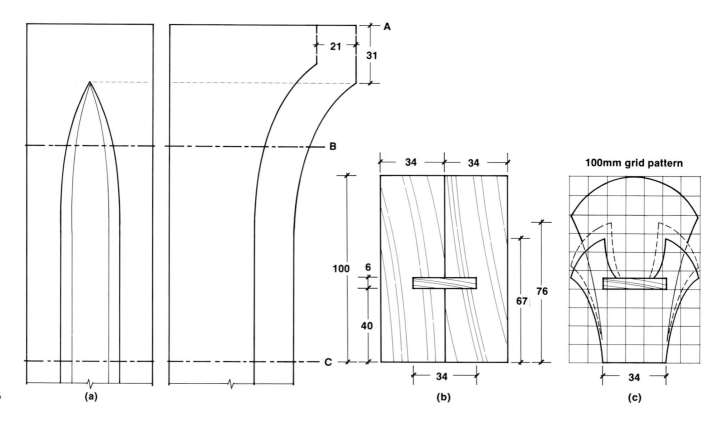

(a)  (b)  (c)

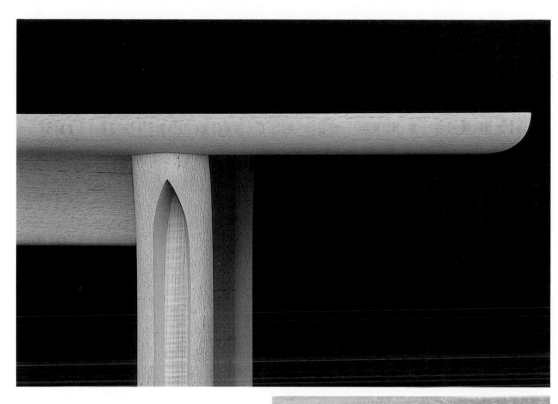

**Above and below: details of side table.**
Photographer: John McCormick.

## Assembly and finishing

• Sand rails and pedestals ready for assembly. Glue rails to pedestals using dowels and cramp lightly with sash cramps or straps. Allow glue to dry. Glue in corner blocks and allow glue to dry.

• Place the table top upside down and locate the pedestals in their correct position. Mark out the recess to be removed from the underside of the table edges to accommodate the pedestals. Remove the waste using chisel and gouge.

• Sand all members to a final finish. Apply two coats of ammonia and hydrogen peroxide and wash all surfaces well with clean water. Allow to dry thoroughly.

• Apply two coats of polyurethane sanding sealer followed by two coats of satin wax. Both these products were chosen as, unlike most lacquers, they do not give a yellow colouring to the timber.

• Assemble the table top and pedestals using the timber buttons.

Before the advent of modern machinery, most of the north coast of New South Wales was part of the 'big scrub', a not-too-affectionate name for the dense forests which grew in each river valley. In those days the giant trees resisted in a protracted battle the axes and willpower of the men who cleared the forest for timber or dairy farms. Because of the timber still milled in these valleys and the high cost of workshop space in the cities, many woodworkers have migrated to share the lifestyle and beauty of these forests. Michael Gill and Chris Payne are new arrivals to the Manning Valley, five hours' drive from the pounding traffic, theatres, restaurants and coffee shops of inner-city Sydney. Neither has the inclination to farm, to run stock or to squeeze a 'battler's' dollar from an abused and misunderstood land. They are there for the clean air and the birds and animals in the 40 acres of native forest of Plum Pudding Brush.

Michael is a graphic artist, woodcarver and sculptor who combines all these talents in furniture. Chris is an illustrator specialising in plantlife. Both treasured the culture and excitement of city life, but they have a new vision for Plum Pudding Brush. Their property is near the end of a valley behind Tinonee, a dot on the map west of Taree. At the time I visited there was no need for a gate because the 10-metre wooden bridge crossing Plum Pudding Creek into their property was still to be finished, and it required a sure step across support logs to enter. A caravan parked beneath a brush shelter, a terrace made from rough-sawn boards, another shelter for the smithy, a compost toilet open to the elements and neat firewood stacks are all that have yet been built. The morning was cool, but the summers in these back valleys can be stifling, and the striped shade cast by the shelter looked inviting.

Bird sounds are everywhere. The hillside is heavily wooded and the creek below the camp is dense with lily pilly brush. Michael and Chris have cleared a space for their future home and studio on the crest of the hill. There is a wide view of the valley to the north, and a dense timber backdrop to the south. The ground floor studio/workshop will contain accommodation for students of the courses in woodcarving and

**Michael Gill on his bridge to Plum Pudding Brush.**
Photographer: Chris Payne.

sculpture, bush furniture making, woodcut printing, papermaking and botanical illustration which Michael and Chris intend to conduct. Students who attended their courses in Sydney and enjoyed Chris's cooking would find a course in this beautiful setting even more inviting.

Their friends are bemused by their move to the bush. After visiting their previous residence-cum-workshop in an old factory on one of the busiest interurban roads in Sydney, many friends could not understand why a naturalist and woodcarver would live and work in such a thunderously disturbing environment. Here Michael created some of the most beautiful native forms carved in Australia and Chris spent each day in her studio at the National Herbarium in Sydney's Botanic Gardens, only to return in the evening to that groaning concrete jungle. They are no less confident in the strange environment of Tinonee than before. In this new setting he still displays all the attributes of a professional craftsman, although recently the public has heard more of him on national radio talking about conservation issues than they have seen exhibitions of his work. His furniture and carvings are still sought for exhibitions, commissioned by museums, public buildings and private homes. He has also been guest lecturer and artist in residence at the Canberra School of Art.

Michael Gill has an independence of spirit, and consequently of product, which is the envy of fellow woodworkers. He still makes only those furniture pieces or sculptures for which he feels a passionate compulsion. Recently that same position led him to spend six months researching the *Good Wood Guide*, a book which he and other timber-using professionals were hopeful would change people's attitudes to forest management. He hopes, once established at Plum Pudding Brush, to return to a partly finished cabinet of mammoth proportions on which he has already worked for 18 months. The financial security provided by teaching has ensured that major pieces like this cabinet can be undertaken without worrying 'will it sell?'. He *knows* that eventually it will. This freedom has allowed Michael to work on pieces which continually expand the boundaries of his craft.

'I have acquired my woodworking skills without a single formal lesson,' he says. 'It has all come through books, experimentation, contact with other woodworkers and the need to make. I would have probably learnt much more rapidly if I'd been formally taught, but by critically analysing failures, successes and processes I've found out what works for me. Being self-taught, I think I'm a more understanding teacher and it's given my work a quality which I believe is distinctive.'

Like other craftspeople, he has found that other skills needed for success have been just as difficult to learn. 'Some designers make beautiful work which doesn't sell, then fret about not being appreciated. If it's designed *to sell* and then doesn't, something is very wrong. In that respect I suppose I'm some sort of businessman. A strong sense of good popular taste is an indispensable design skill *if* you want to sell. The great problem when you are establishing yourself is that you have to be good at everything; designing, making and selling. It's demoralising having your own workshop and biting your fingernails all day worrying about money. I made the resolution early in my career to be good at working in wood, to ensure my work was respected and not to hide in a cupboard. That sounds cocksure and smug, but heads are ridiculous things with which to bang brick walls and I'm not such a stolid slogger by nature.'

Michael admits that his greatest problem was learning about wood; to assess the quality of figure and colour in a rough-sawn board; to gauge the suitability and degree of seasoning of timber for a project, then how to cut it sympathetically and to dress it with a finish that gives it a second life.

'The successful woodworker needs to be able to talk confidently about his or her art, and perhaps even to write. A lack of confidence in any of these produces problems. If these skills aren't native they can be learnt, consciously developed, or handed over to professionals.'

Although he believes that design is not totally inherited, he confides that his maternal grandfather was a set designer for the National Opera in Budapest, and his paternal great-grandfather a watchmaker and jeweller in London. Michael has always drawn, and disliked school enough to leave early to study art at the East Sydney Technical College. The world of advertising which followed college was unsatisfying. It was antique furniture and the framing of his own work which first introduced Michael to wood. He set up a simple workshop in his lounge room and was launched, rolling and pitching, on a new career. Four years of travel, work and study overseas fed the conviction that making beautiful things in a beautiful medium was a fine way to try to make a living.

Michael describes himself on his letterhead as a 'Designer-Maker', and his work bears the mark of his graphic skill. Decoration is a distinctive feature of all his work in the form of carving, marquetry or inlay, which are important parts of the total design in each piece. He feels strongly that decoration has been overlooked and often denigrated in modern furniture design.

'Decoration disappeared from much furniture-making after World War II. Function and form have reigned supreme since. Engineering considerations have been dominant, and designers have been absorbed by the problems of stress analysis

*Mitch* — **a woman In love with a Major Mitchell cockatoo, life-size in Huon pine.** Photographer: Bill Anagrius.

and function. This is as it should be, but we not only physically use furniture. We live with it and look at it, and surely it can say something more to us. The Scandinavians emphasised a structurally sculptured form to the exclusion of almost all else. We shouldn't blinker ourselves to the potential of decoration. In Victorian times it took a great deal of courage *not* to decorate furniture. It now takes courage to incorporate it sensitively. I like to use many woodcutting skills and to enhance each piece with decoration, where it makes sense to me. Not just icing on the cake — it must have some intrinsic merit, or express a mood. Sometimes it's just good fun to stick in a wild-eyed cockatoo or to inlay some mother-of-pearl that shimmers like moonlit clouds.'

Michael's sculptures range from a cicada and leaf pattern brooch only 65mm across to *Mitch*, a life-size Huon pine punk bust, a portrait of a woman in love with a Major Mitchell cockatoo. 'She is a *decorated* person, far more committed to this form of self-expression than simply painting on eye-liner, red lippy and a blue rinse.' His small pieces are precisely carved, many having a circular configuration, a dominant feature of his decorative details.

Chris and Michael collaborate constantly on all their work. She shares his interest in the conservation movement as well as his determination to change government and public attitudes to promote responsible harvesting of forests and the mixed planting of native species. Since their involvement in researching and writing for the conservation movement, their opinions, knowledge and experience of forest management have been refined. It is a sad tale that they relate: 'Every commercial species has been consistently over-cut, some depleted to the extent that they're no longer anything more than icons, historical and ecological memories. Export of timber on a large scale has been a constant drain on the resources of this country for 200 years. You can find carriages

**Brooch of blackwood leaves and flowers in mulberry and Tasmanian blackwood, 65mm diameter, 12mm deep.** Photographer: Michael Gill.

**Cicada brooch — Australian purple heart acacia wings, transparent membrane in casting resin and onyx eyes, 100mm wingspan.** Photographer: Michael Gill.

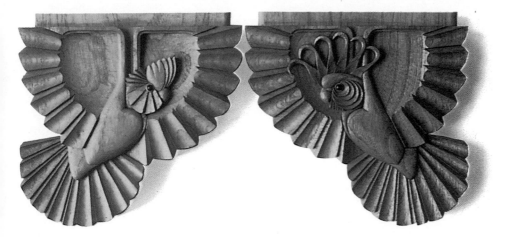

**Shelf brackets — each face is carved with a different Australian bird. Shown, the galah and Major Mitchell cockatoo, 260mm high and 40mm thick.**
Photographer: Michael Gill.

on the London Underground panelled and lined in silky oak from Queensland rainforests, staircases in the USA of black bean, and our north coast hardwoods in railway sleepers in India. Today, millions of tonnes of forest leave our shores as woodchips, bound largely for Japan.

'Even our plantation woods have been established by first destroying natural forests. This is taking one step forward and two steps back. To have any real effect on the management of our forests, we now know that we have to get angry and vent that anger politically. As a low-volume, high value-added consumer of wood, it's easier for me to use it and still get a good night's sleep. I now buy only selectively logged regrowth, refusing anything associated with clear felling, woodchipping or old growth logging. My suppliers, luckily, are understanding and honest. If I use rainforest woods, they are chainsaw milled on the forest floor from trees that have been brought down by wind or died of natural causes.

'I'm looking forward to milling more of my own timber using my chainsaw, which weighs more than I do. It will be good to know my wood in the log rather than buying it ready-sawn.

'I'm looking forward to building my own workshop, studio and house, and hope it will be as satisfying as building this great bridge has been.

'I'm looking forward to designing and making all our own furniture, and to planting thousands of native trees on this place and leaving it as an arboretum to people who love and value such things.

'I'm looking forward to teaching my private classes again and meeting students from overseas and Australia.'

Perhaps Chris and Michael are more articulate than those who originally settled this land, but they probably share similar aspirations to make the good life in their own terms. We all have our own sense of creation and creativity, whether it be cutting down or planting trees or both. Hopefully, we can learn from the mistakes of our forebears as they did from theirs.

# Settle

**M**ichael Gill designed the first of these settles in 1985 for the Australian furniture collection at the Powerhouse Museum in Sydney and for the New Parliament House, Canberra. A number of settles of this design have subsequently been made, each in different timbers. The settle described here is made from Australian red cedar, with inlays and contrasting strips of Huon pine. One is a close-grained rich red, the other a soft honey-coloured timber. Although the contrast in these timbers is extreme, it need not be so. Michael has made a settle from silky oak and beefwood, timbers with contrasting colours but similar texture and grain, with prominent medullary rays.

It is interesting to examine the original drawings Michael made for the first settle. These included numerous sketches of alternatives for joining the members. Furniture made from solid timber must be constructed to allow for across-grain expansion and contraction of any large members. The seat and the 'fretted forest' back can pose particular problems in this regard. Although you may wish to alter the detailing and modify the joints, it would be wise to follow Michael's solution to allow for movement in these members. The original fretted forest was designed in collaboration with Christine Payne, and is a clever solution to allow for movement by breaking up the backrest into individual panels. Read carefully the explanation on

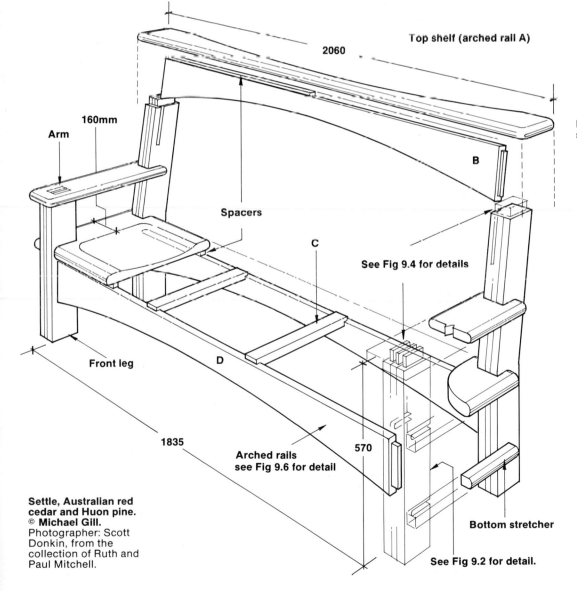

Fig 9.1 Anatomy of the settle.

Top shelf (arched rail A)

2060

160mm

Arm

B

Spacers

See Fig 9.4 for details

C

Front leg

D

1835

Arched rails
see Fig 9.6 for detail

570

Bottom stretcher

See Fig 9.2 for detail.

Settle, Australian red cedar and Huon pine.
© Michael Gill.
Photographer: Scott Donkin, from the collection of Ruth and Paul Mitchell.

how these panels should be fixed to the arched frame and the seat to prevent them from splitting.

The settle is large, with an overall length of 2060mm, but does not appear massive in its finished form, due to careful shaping and detailing. You will notice that all vertical members are left with the arris intact while all horizontal members have the edges fully rounded. If any of these details are altered, you should consider the effect these changes may have on the final appearance of the settle. The choice of timbers for the leg and the inlay is important as the legs are large in section, 115mm x 82mm. The timbers chosen should provide sufficient contrast to produce a distinct banded effect on the front edge, reducing the visual weight of the leg. To assess whether your choice of timber will achieve the desired effect, it would be best to make a prototype of a front leg before proceeding with the construction. Michael Gill used urea formaldehyde to glue the widening joints, and epoxy resin glue, which has a slow rate of set-up, for all structural joints.

# Making the settle

In Michael Gill's settle the seat is a structural member jointed to both the back and front legs. End frames are formed by the front and back legs, the arm and the bottom stretcher. This jointed frame enables the seat to be glued to the back leg, but the joint between the seat and the front leg is **not** glued, to allow for movement. The seat is slot-screwed through bearers below to fix the seat to the structure. The legs are jointed to the arched rails, the seat and the top shelf. This interlocking construction provides a very strong structure. To ensure that the distances between joints are marked accurately, a working rod, a full-sized drawing of the side view shown in Fig 9.2, should be made on a sheet of plywood. It may also help to make a working rod of a front view, showing the distances between shoulders on the arched rails and the position of joints on the seat.

## Making the legs

• If you have timber 75mm thick from which to make the legs, you may wish to match the colour and grain of this timber with that of the planks selected for the other members. If not, arrange the timber to achieve a deliberate contrast in tone, colour and grain to show the range of natural variations in your chosen species. Prepare the front legs to sectional size 110mm x 75mm and cut to lengths of 575mm, which will allow a 5mm horn on the tenons protruding through the top surface of the arm. The shape of the back leg should be set out from the working rod of the side view. Place the finished back leg on the drawing and check that the angle formed by the front edges perfectly matches the angle marked on the rod.

• Cut a 15mm wide groove down the centre of the front edge of the front and back legs to a depth of 10mm, using a straight bit in a router. Glue in the contrasting inlays (in this case Huon pine) cut from 5mm thick timber and cramp

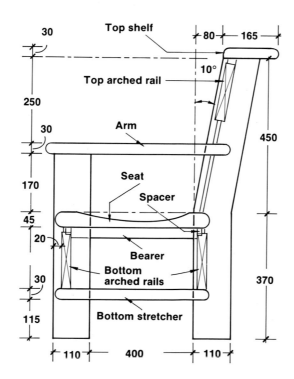

Fig 9.2 Side view of the settle, showing detailed dimensions.

Top shelf
30
80 — 165
10°
Top arched rail
250
30
Arm
450
170
Seat
Spacer
45
20
Bearer
Bottom arched rails
30
370
115
Bottom stretcher
110    400    110

lightly until dry. Note that the inlay is recessed 5mm below the front edge of each leg to produce a shadow line, as shown in Fig 9.3.

• If timber of 75mm thickness is not available, the legs can be made from three laminates, as shown in Fig 9.3. The contrasting centre laminate is recessed 5mm below the front edge of each leg to produce a shadow line.

• Plane a 4mm chamfer on the bottom ends of all legs.

## Making the arms

• Prepare the two arms to sectional size 150mm x 30mm and cut each to a length of 545mm.

• The multiple mortice and tenon joint between the front leg and arm is shown in Fig 9.4. If the leg is made from solid timber, the centre tenon is shortened or omitted entirely and the open mortice on the top face of the arm filled with an inlay of the contrasting timber. If the legs are made from laminations, three through tenons are used, with the centre tenon being from the contrasting timber. The position of the mortice on the arm and the shoulder of the tenon on the leg should be marked directly from the working rod.

• The joint between the arm and the back leg is shown in Fig 9.2 and is a type of stopped bridle joint, similar to that used between the seat and the back leg, but with an angled shoulder to match the slope of the back leg. The angled trenches on the back leg should be set out by placing the back leg and arm in position over the working rod. The shoulder of the joint on the arm can be marked at the same time.

## Making the bottom stretchers

• Prepare the two bottom stretchers to sectional size 120mm x 30mm and cut to a length of 450mm.

• The joint is a simple through

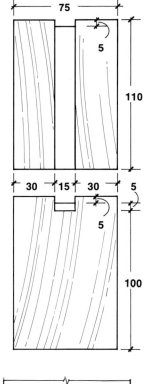

Fig 9.3 Alternative methods of shaping or laminating the legs.

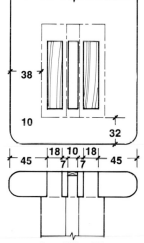

Leg 100 x 75

Fig 9.4 Details of the mortice and tenon between the arm and front leg.

tongue and trench as shown in Fig 9.5. The shoulders on the bottom stretchers should be marked directly from the working rod.

## Making the seat

• The seat is 450mm wide, is made from two planks of approximately equal width and is edge-glued. As the seat is shaped as shown in Fig 9.6, any dowel, spline or biscuit used in joining these two planks will need to be offset as the seat is only 15mm thick at the joint. The

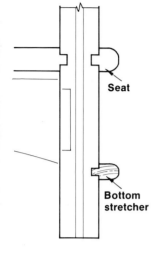

Fig 9.5 Section of the front leg.

Seat

Bottom stretcher

two planks should be thicknessed to 45mm before jointing, and two edges planed to form a gap-free joint. After the glue has dried, the seat can be cut to a length of 2060mm.

• To shape the seat, 13 parallel cuts of varying depth are made using a portable circular saw. Each cut should be stopped at a marked line 160mm short of either end of the seat. Waste between the saw cuts can be removed with a gouge and mallet. The bottom of each saw kerf provides a depth gauge in shaping the seat. The surface is finally shaped and finished across the grain using a fine (No. 7) gouge. Small overlapped cuts with a very sharp gouge will produce a dimpled surface which should only require very light sanding.

• The joints between the seat and the front and back legs are shown in Fig 9.5, and are similar to those used between the arm and the back leg. The distance between the shoulders of this joint, measured across the seat, is identical to that between the shoulders of the bottom stretcher. Mark out the corresponding half of these joints on the front and back legs, using the rod of the side view to mark the position of the joint.

## Making the top shelf

• Prepare the top shelf to sectional size 165mm x 30mm and cut to a length of 2060mm. Mark the shape of the top shelf A, as shown in the template in Fig 9.7. Cut the curve and dress the edge. This curve can be used as a template to mark identical curves on the three arched rails, B, C and D.

• The joint between the top shelf and back legs is a multiple mortice and tenon joint identical to that used in the arm to front leg joint. The setting out of this joint and its cutting are as described previously, and sizes are shown in Fig 9.4.

## Making the arched rails

• The three arched rails are identical in size and shape. Prepare the three arched rails to sectional size 165mm x 30mm and cut each to a length of 1875mm.

• The joints between the two lower arched rails and the legs are common stopped mortice and tenons 60mm in depth. Note that the mortice between the top arched rail and the back leg is open to the top end of the leg and is only 5mm deep, to allow for assembly of the top arch rail over the forest panel.

• Using the curve on the top shelf

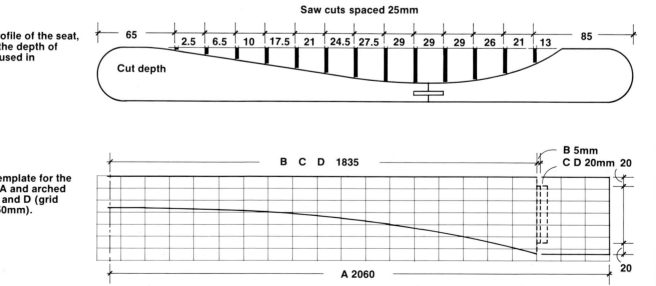

Fig 9.6 Profile of the seat, showing the depth of saw cuts used in shaping.

Saw cuts spaced 25mm

65    2.5  6.5  10  17.5  21  24.5  27.5  29  29  29  26  21  13    85

Cut depth

Fig 9.7 Template for the top shelf A and arched rails B, C and D (grid 25mm x 50mm).

B C D  1835

B 5mm
C D 20mm  20

A 2060

20

as a template, mark out the curve on each of the arched rails and cut these curves and dress the edges.

## Making the bearers and spacers

• Two bearers must be made to join the front and back arched rails and to support the underside of the seat. Prepare these to sectional size 55mm x 30mm and cut to a length of 395mm. Simple lapped joints are made on either end. Note in Fig 9.8 that the laps do not extend to the outer face of the arched rails and are hidden by spacers. Counterbore and drill the holes in the underside of each bearer for the slip screws.

• The three spacers are made from the contrasting timber, in this case Huon pine. Prepare the spacers which fit beneath the seat to sectional size, 25mm x 15mm, and cut to a length of 1830mm, which allows a little waste to be removed from one end in the final fitting. The spacer to fit between the arched rail and the top shelf is 30mm wide and shaped to close the gap between these two members when the settle is assembled as in the end view. The spacers will be glued and screwed to the top edge of the arched rails 5mm from the front face of each rail to provide a shadow line on the final assembly.

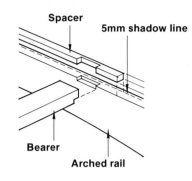

Spacer

5mm shadow line

Bearer

Arched rail

Fig 9.8 Detail of bearer and spacer attached to back arched rail.

Mark out and cut the shape of each tree panel allowing for a 10mm long stub tenon, as shown in Fig 9.9. Decorative inlays of birds can be placed amongst the trees. Michael Gill cut these from 3mm thick Huon pine, and they depict yellow tailed black cockatoos.

• Assemble the top arched rail and seat to the back legs and cramp lightly in place. The bottom edges of the trees can now be fitted to the surface of the seat to give a gap-free joint. Holding each tree panel in position, mark the arc from the underside of the arched rail on the top of each panel. Mark the position of the corresponding mortice on the underside of the arched rail. Mark also the location of the dowels used to join the bottom of the trees to the seat.

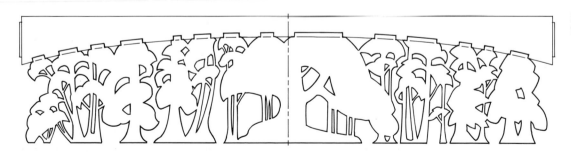

Fig 9.9 Profile of the forest back panel.

## Making the forest panels

• The panels of trees are made from red cedar boards dressed to 20mm thick. The large centre panel is made from six edge-glued boards approximately 150mm wide.

• Disassemble the members and complete the marking-out of mortices on the under edge of the arched rail and the centres for the dowels on the surface of the seat. Chop the mortices. Drill holes for the 20mm x 6mm diameter dowels used to joint the bottom of the trees to the seat. Shape the stub tenons and reassemble the members for a final fitting.

## Final shaping and assembly

• The edges of all horizontal members are to be rounded, and this can be done using a router and a 15mm round over bit.

• Ensure that all joints fit well and

carry out a trial assembly.

• Disassemble the members and sand all surfaces of each member to a final finish.

• Glue and screw the spacer to the top edge of the front arched rail and trim to length. Glue the arched rails to the front legs and cramp lightly until the glue is dry, ensuring that the members are square.

**Detail of forest panel.**
Photographer: Scott Donkin.

• Glue the bottom arched rails to the back legs and check that the leg is square with the upper edge of the rail before cramping lightly. Leave until the glue is dry.

• Glue the bearers into the back arched rail beneath the seat. Glue the arms to the front legs and, after applying glue to the remaining joints, slide the front and back assemblies together. **Note that the joints between the front edge of the seat and the front legs are not glued, nor are the bearers glued to the underside of the seat. If these joints are glued, the seat will split with movement.** Finally glue the bottom stretchers to front and back legs. Cramp all joints lightly and allow glue to cure.

• Glue and screw the spacer to the top arched rail and trim to length.

• Apply glue **only** to the centre dowels and to the centre of each stub tenon on the forest panels to allow the panels to expand and contract. Locate the dowels in their corresponding holes in the seat and fix the forest panels in their correct position. These panels should be held in position relative to each other by cramping narrow battens across the full face of the panels. Apply glue to the mortice and tenon joints between the top arched rail and back legs, and slide this member vertically into position over the stub tenons on the forest panels. Complete the assembly by gluing the top shelf to the back leg and the arched rail. Cramp the complete assembly, and allow glue to cure.

• Dress off the exposed tenons on the arms and the top shelf, and fine sand all surfaces with 400 grit.

• Michael Gill finished the settle using four coats of Danish oil, sanding with 1000 grit wet and dry between and with coats. Fine-grained timbers may demand that the final coat be buffed lightly with fine steel wool prior to polishing with a quality furniture oil.

**Detail of legs and rails.**
Photographer: Scott Donkin.

**Greg Collins with his turned bowls from City of Perth Craft Awards for 1990.**
West Australian Newspapers Ltd.

'They lie like spaceships darkly loitering.' That sentence inexplicably entered my mind as I walked into Greg Collins' workshop and saw in the dull light the flat turned shapes apparently floating above the bench. Beer cans in hand, Greg and a friend, Bob, were talking over trading their services. I soon had a beer as well, and Greg explained the reason for my visit. The friendly banter flowed, and Bob excused himself and left. The workshop was an adaptation on a large shed, built with numerous additions in a mixture of brick, steel and galvanised iron. It was a bitterly cold day for October, and I shivered at the thought of what the workshop must be like in winter. It all looked very businesslike, but it was hard to reconcile the adventurous turned shapes on the bench and their maker, who impressed as a rather impish leprechaun. It took no more than a few minutes to appreciate that I would enjoy talking to this man. His light-hearted manner made me want to share his good humour, while those bowls about the workshop were testimony to his individuality and his eye for shape and form. A designer with something interesting to say.

Why is it that some craftsmen like Greg Collins, who are self-taught, generate designs which are so novel, using techniques which many would consider unsound to the point of being irreligious? I use that word advisedly, because there are some in all crafts who think of themselves as the keepers of wisdom, the formulators of doctrine and defenders of the faith. Then along comes a young bearded man, unpretentious and eloquent, who attacks that faith by not recognising most of its tenets and begins to write a new text based on his experiences of life and his thoughts on what might be. The analogy is possibly mischievous, but there is an element of truth hidden within it. Some untrained craftsmen never create anything of worth, while others who are trained only make what they are taught to recreate. There are those, however, like Greg Collins, who begin with a piece of wood at hand and little else, and create as they learn.

Greg is a product of the hard school of life, an education system not recommended for the faint at heart. He admits to having had a specific learning difficulty at school, and left early

**Greg Collins turning in his workshop.**

to take up whatever work was available. He found he was good with his hands and could somehow make things which other people found difficult. An acquaintance asked him to make a cabinet and he agreed, not having any useful tools or knowing how it could be built. That was a sign of supreme confidence or blind faith in his own ability. The cabinet was built, the friend was satisfied with the job, and Greg was off on the road to becoming one of the most noted woodworkers of Western Australia. Eventually he realised that he needed to know more and enrolled at Curtin University as a mature student to study design, but found that those problems he had experienced at school would prevent him finishing the course. That shortens and romanticises the tale, because there were periods of despair and times of anguish and distress before he settled with his wife and two children in Margaret River, 200km south of Perth, a renowned wine-growing area with wonderful surfing beaches besides.

When talking to Greg, with his unruly beard, tousled hair and ebullient manner, you could be excused for thinking you were with an Irish bard. The voice is well-modulated and the vowels rounded, the hands move incessantly and argument is incisive. Obviously if you have a quick intelligence, life is a good teacher.

He began with furniture, simple pieces at first, but with each came greater confidence and a more ambitious design. Not knowing the limits of the timber you work with can produce some disasters, like tables which disintegrate with the first change of weather. He now knows to allow for movement in solid timber, but it was not the only harsh lesson to be borne with humility. Soon it became obvious that he could not survive without a product which would provide a cash flow. He had inherited a simple lathe from his grandfather, along with a set of equally simple tools, and he taught himself to turn. Surprisingly, people bought whatever he made, and he had solved yet another problem. His skills improved with each piece, and he was soon exhibiting with other professionals. Months after holding his first one-man show he won the 1984 City of Perth Craft Award, one of the most prestigious awards in Australia.

With this public recognition came the ambition to promote his work in the eastern states and overseas. To listen to the saga of misadventures which followed is to appreciate Greg's qualities and foibles. If a table springs apart when in a gallery, that is a problem, but his early forays in marketing were unmitigated disasters. Both were valuable learning experiences and have been treated as such, put aside but not forgotten. To listen to Greg and his wife Sandi talk about that time in their life is to feel heartened by the resilience of the human spirit.

They laugh uproariously about Greg's bad fortune and mistakes, and make light of its legacy.

'I was asked to exhibit by an agent,' he relates, 'who had contacts in Tokyo. Although I should have been sceptical about his credentials and his appearance was rather strange, I thought the opportunity was too good to miss. I presented a large number of pieces, and the exhibition, held in a first-class hotel, went very well, with me selling eight bowls in the first two days. One was bought by the Australian Embassy. The asking price was at least five times what I would have received in Australia, and I was over the moon. I went off to *ikebana* classes to study the types of bowls which would be best suited to the market in Japan. I took it all very seriously, but after one week it became obvious that expenses were going to sink any profit I might make from the venture. Standing up and breathing are very expensive pastimes in Tokyo, so I left my remaining bowls with the agent and returned home. That was the last I heard of him or my stock. In a way the loss of those bowls wasn't as bitter as knowing there was a market there which I hadn't been able to tap. I simply came back and started all over again. I've always been a bit like a knight charging on a white steed, with a bowl in each hand. I don't think I'll ever be any different.'

He returned with the resolve to get it right next time. Greg had printed professional brochures of his work and wrote overseas to gauge the reaction. He attended seminars run by Austrade, and learned more about promoting himself overseas and making financial transactions.

'The Trade and Development Department of the Western Australian Government was organising an exhibition in Hong Kong, and they invited me to be involved. I applied for grants from the State Arts Department and the Fine Wood Project, and with some of my own money I financed the trip. I put together some of my best work ever, bought a business suit, striped tie, Italian shoes and a briefcase, and was off to Hong Kong. Not only did I look the part, but was given star billing at the exhibition. It was a huge success. Within two days I had sold the whole exhibition, had orders worth $24,000 and organised for a local interior designer to act as my agent. The Hilton Hotel bought half my exhibition pieces for their executive suites. The agent had import and export divisions in his company, and I returned home and airfreighted back $12,000 worth of stock. I later went to the Milan Furniture Fair, confident that all was well. I returned home via Hong Kong, did radio and TV interviews, and then the wheel fell off! The principals of the export division of the agent's company absconded to the USA with my bowls. There was so much bitterness in the company that all deals were off, and a long and expensive legal battle began over ownership of those bowls.

*Inner Space*, **pink ivory wood, African ebony, MDF with textured blackboy veneers, 250mm x 250mm x 210mm.**
Photographer: Victor France.

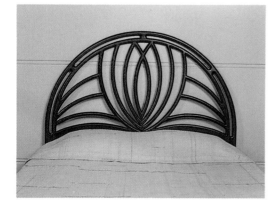

***Outer Space*, she-oak, African ebony, black lacquered MDF, 600mm diameter x 90mm.**
Photographer: Victor France.

**Bedhead, laminated jarrah, 150 pieces.**
Photographer: Greg Collins.

Although I had filled the orders taken at the exhibition and completed commissions for the Hong Kong Club, I had lost money. On the prospect of all that work I had put on staff, built a bigger lathe and gone into debt. It was a disaster!'

What does a person like Greg Collins do when a year's work has gone for naught and he is nearly insolvent? Work harder, of course. What else is there to do? He is still working very long hours, hoping to overcome that disaster in his life, yet Sandi and he often laugh in telling of their naiveté and misfortune.

Greg won a Churchill Fellowship in 1989, and travelled throughout the USA visiting workshops and galleries to assess the viability of marketing there. With greater caution and certainty he is now working on pieces for an exhibition at a gallery in Philadelphia. With no illusions about the difficulty of making a name in that country, his approach is much more cautious and conservative.

He is applying the same principles to marketing his work in the eastern states of Australia. Greg has entered into an agreement with a local marketing agent to display in Sydney galleries. He admits, 'I'm now far more cautious than in my Hong Kong venture. I've never been interested in money. It's the challenge of getting whatever I do right. There has to be more to it than making the next piece; I'd soon get bored if that was all there was to designing and making. With all of my work, I try to ensure it's sold before I make it, and so far I've been successful. So to me, promoting my work and marketing it properly is just as important as making it.'

His success at producing marketable work is the envy of most woodworkers in Western Australia. Greg Collins is bemused by woodturners or furniture designer-makers who find difficulty in selling their work. He professes not to worry whether his work will sell, and is always confident that it will. Nor does he make pieces to a marketing formula. The shapes he generates are creations of his own genius, and he delights in continually moving off in new directions, sure that if it looks right to his eye it is certain to appeal to others. His judgement in this is uncanny, as the bowls he creates are not extraordinary, but the amalgam of shape, texture, grain pattern, colour and finish makes the work distinctive. He delights in doing the unusual in composites, but his touch is so sure that his pieces have a signature of their own.

Greg recognises that the market for one-off commissioned furniture in Western Australia is very small, and transport costs to the eastern states make competing with other designer-makers very difficult. He admits that he couldn't meet his commitments if he were to rely on making furniture alone. There are many furniture makers working in the south-west of

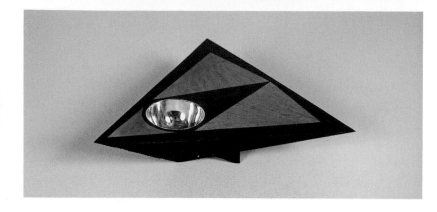

**_Sterling In Space_, mallee burl, African ebony, textured and ebonised blackboy, MDF.** Photographer: Greg Collins.

GREG COLLINS

the state, but most are content to make standard designs of tables, chairs and cabinets and rely on the quality of the timber, rather than the beauty of the design, to sell the piece. This Greg finds frustrating, as the timber deserves better interpreters than those currently using it. He has been involved in negotiations with the timber industry and government departments on providing value-added industries and craft workshops associated with the timber industry. He and others were instrumental in the introduction of forest-produce craft licences, which entitled woodworkers to salvage fallen timber from the forest for a small fee. Greg sites the instance of a fallen jarrah log which was to be burnt as it was unsuitable for commercial milling. From that log he made furniture and bowls with a wholesale value at $30,000. Most woodworkers sensibly advertise their work as being made from fallen timber.

Many of his most recent 'spaceship bowls' have been made from medium density fibre board (MDF). The body of the shape is made from this composite board, and the edge is banded with 3mm thick veneers of forest oak and ebony. The exposed surfaces of MDF are ribbed and lacquered black to give a sharp contrast to the brightly coloured segments of timber. The crown is hollowed to receive a small bowl made from the same timber as that used to veneer the rim. These 'squashed sphere' hollow formed bowls are made from locally harvested hardwoods such as jarrah, jarrah burl, she-oak, grass tree and marri. For furniture panels Greg principally uses veneers glued to a composite board core. He cuts most of the veneer himself from specially selected stock. Greg is fastidious in finishing timber, using the same process as that employed in the motor industry.

I left Greg Collins regretting that I had not seen him turn one of his huge bowls on his equally huge lathe. Most of his tools are self-made adaptations of cutters used on a metal lathe. No doubt aesthetes of woodturning would cringe in horror, but the shape and finish are there to prove that they work. Most woodworkers would be challenged to review their practices by watching Greg in action. It may be that we all develop our own style in working with wood and a belief in what is _right_ — the best do, I am sure.

# Silver Eye Display Table

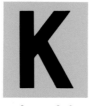 **K**eeping an open mind about what a table made from timber should look like is a problem shared by designer-makers and clients. To break free of the confines of the material is the intent of some woodworkers and the hope of others. Most who study and appreciate fine wooden furniture look for the intrinsic properties of the timber to contribute to the appeal of a piece, while others make or purchase with this factor as the prime or sole consideration.

With the Silver Eye table, Greg Collins is presenting a study in contrasts of textures and finish. It is a disarmingly simple table in form and structure, but on closer examination it says something about Western Australia and the obsession some woodworkers have with grain, colour and timber quality, to the exclusion of all else. Those who know Greg expect a cryptic 'comment', as his designs will often defy convention and compel a rethink of former precepts.

The centre panel in the top of this table is made from veneers cut from an olive tree planted by Sir John Forrest, an early explorer of Western Australia and its first Premier. The tree had grown on Sir John's farm in Picton, near Bunbury, and had died before Greg Collins' chainsaw milled it eight years ago. It was extremely hard and close-grained, and was capable of being finished to a mirror-like surface.

Greg also acquired a giant grass tree and, instead of using this to turn bowls as he had on many occasions, decided to experiment by cutting veneers from this strange timber. This plant grows throughout Australia, and is known variously as blackboy or *Xanthorrhosa Australia*. In the eastern states it grows only on sandstone ridges, but in Western Australia it grows widely throughout the south-west, wherever there are sandy soils, and can grow to the size of a small tree. Discovered recently by woodturners for its unusual open grain, it has been harvested to the point of protection in many areas. It has little structural strength but has a strong medullary ray pattern, with large open pores towards its outer surface. Greg considered it would provide a startling contrast to other timbers if used in a table.

## Making the table

The Silver Eye table is unique because of the timbers and finishes Greg Collins has used. It should be possible, however, to emulate the contrasts of colours and textures. Any dense, close-grained timber such as olive would be suitable for the centre panel on the top. The edging surrounding this panel is made from silver beech finished with an ebony stain. Ebonising on silver beech gives a uniform slate black colour which, if unfilled, provides a contrast of colour and texture to the olive wood centre panel. Any timber which has similar characteristics to silver beech can be used for the edging and should produce the same effect.

What of the legs? Where do you acquire a Western Australian grass tree? As the amount of timber needed for these veneers is quite small, they could be cut from any small fast-growing tree or shrub. *Banksia ericifolia* will yield veneers with large irregular medullary rays and a very open grain. While not possessing the chaotic grain pattern of the grass tree, if finished as described here, the effect would be at least superficially similar. The challenge in making this table is not necessarily in the construction, but in choosing timbers which will give a similar effect to that achieved by Greg Collins.

**Silver Eye display table.**
© **Greg Collins.**
Photographer: Greg Collins.

**Detail of table.**
Photographer: Greg Collins.

109

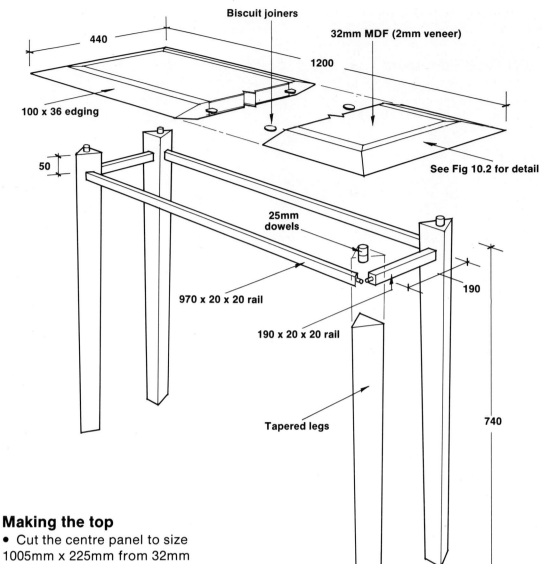

**Fig 10.1 Anatomy of Silver Eye display table.**

Biscuit joiners

32mm MDF (2mm veneer)

440

1200

100 x 36 edging

See Fig 10.2 for detail

50

25mm dowels

190

970 x 20 x 20 rail

190 x 20 x 20 rail

Tapered legs

740

## Making the top

• Cut the centre panel to size 1005mm x 225mm from 32mm MDF board.

• Cut the veneers to 3mm thickness using a close-grained feature timber for the top surface (olive wood). A commercial close-grained veneer can be used for the underside (kauri). Edge-join the veneers and tape to form a panel.

• Glue with a two-pot epoxy and press the veneers to the core. When dry, trim and dress the faces of the veneers. Dress the panel edges to give a finished size of 1000mm x 220mm.

• Prepare the silver beech edging to sectional size 100mm x 36mm. Cut the timber to form the mitre joints and set out and cut the biscuit joints in the positions shown in the exploded perspective drawing. Mark the 65mm wide double splay and plane the splay, leaving a little waste to be removed

**Fig 10.2 Section of table top showing details of edging.**

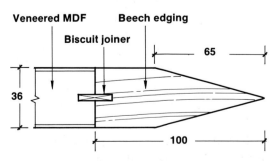

Veneered MDF

Beech edging

Biscuit joiner

65

36

100

to form the final edge when the top is assembled.

• Glue the edging to the centre panel and cramp lightly. When dry, dress off the centre panel and edging to a flush surface and complete the planing of the splay to form a sharp edge.

## Making the legs

• Prepare the core timber for the legs to sectional shape and size (any straight-grained timber can be used). Each leg is in the shape of an equilateral triangle with 70mm sides. Cut the legs to a length of 760mm. Drill a hole in the centre of the top end of each leg for a 25mm dowel. Each face on the leg is to taper 1° from top to bottom. Mark the taper of 13mm on the foot of each leg, which will give an equilateral triangle with sides of approximately 55mm, and plane the taper.

• Cut the veneers to size and, gluing one face at a time, glue each veneer to the leg. Trim the edges of each veneer before proceeding with the next.

• Mark out the position of the triangular recesses on the faces of the front legs to receive the 25mm sterling silver pyramid inserts, and cut these to fit.

## Making the rails

• Prepare the rails to sectional size 20mm x 20mm from kauri. Cut to lengths of 985mm and 195mm. The ends of the 985mm front and back rails have to be cut at an angle to match the face of the leg.

• Mark out the position of the dowels to form the dowelled butt joints between the rails and the legs. Drill for a 40mm x 12mm diameter dowel and fit the joints.

## Assembly and finishing

• The grass tree veneered legs are textured using a wire brush, and are not sanded.

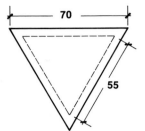

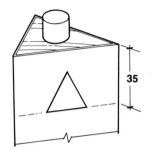

**Fig 10.3 Details of leg.**

Leg tapers 1° top to bottom

View of leg top shows
25mm dowel and position
of silver pyramid

• Sand all remaining surfaces to a final finish.

• Glue and assemble the legs and rails using a two-pot epoxy, and cramp lightly.

• Mark out the position of the dowel holes in the underside of the table aligned with the holes in the top end of each leg. Bore for a 40mm x 25mm diameter dowel.

• Apply the ebony stain to the border, rails and legs, and allow to dry.

Silver Eye display table.
Photographer: Greg Collins.

• Glue the table top to the legs and finish sand all surfaces.

• The table top is finished with a two-pot lacquer with a 25% gloss finish.

• Glue the sterling silver pyramids into the recesses in the legs.

**Anthony Russo.** Photographer: Peter Greenwood Brown.

**Mark Weichard.** Photographer: Peter Greenwood Brown.

Creative people usually prefer to generate their concepts alone, some asking for the appraisal of others and most leaving it to the marketplace or for clients to pass judgement. Few woodworkers work in partnerships as it requires the forbearance and understanding of a full professional relationship, personal compatibility, honesty and openness, and a willingness to make it work to the benefit of both partners.

Anthony Russo and Mark Weichard have made a success of their partnership in *Orchard Sculpture Design*. On a superficial examination of their work, you could be excused for asking why. In appearance and manner they are as unlike each other as their work: Anthony is slight of build, with a slow smile and retiring manner, while Mark has a mass of black curly hair and beard to match a direct, forceful delivery. They are both confident and articulate, but when they speak, Mark often directs the argument and Anthony provides the qualifying statements and exposition. They rarely present contrary opinions, possibly because the arguments between them have been resolved long ago. Such an odd understanding is also evident in their designs and business management. Conflict of purpose may exist, but in discussion it is not evident, as any statement which challenges a proposition is repudiated with complementary arguments, making debating interesting but difficult. I came away from a visit to their workshop having had a new experience and wondering if I had found a new breed of artist-designer, one who is interested in concepts and making in equal measures.

Sculptures in wood usually require a setting. Grinling Gibbons and Tilman Reimenschneider carved at a time when interiors were made of wood panelling, churches were divided by pierced wood screens and roofing timbers were exposed. Reimenschneider set his gaunt figures of Christ and the Apostles in wooden frames depicting contemporary interiors, while modern wood sculptures are frequently left to battle with settings of stone, glass, steel and plastic, often losing the contest. Mark Weichard is the sculptor of a Christ whose haggard features depict a man afflicted with anguish, a vision of Christ shared by Reimenschneider; but the setting composed

# Anthony Russo & Mark Weichard

**Ceremonial bowl detail, jarrah, rosewood and steel, Mark Weichard.** Photographer: Peter Greenwood Brown.

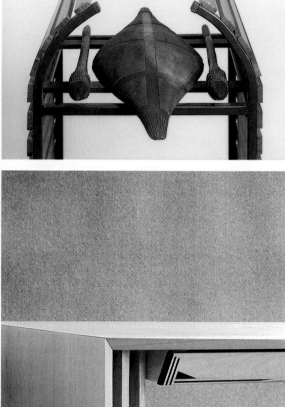

**Side table detail of drawer, silver ash and rosewood inlay, Anthony Russo.** Photographer: Rodney Hyatt.

by Anthony is of the modern world, an architectural landscape of planar surfaces of contrasting line and shadow which complement its dramatic effect perfectly. These backgrounds are fundamental to the whole, and although the elements of carving and setting can be separated in some of their earlier work, most are a unified expression of a single subject. Here we have, not two craftsmen working together, but two minds creating as one. The unity of purpose in this expression is as effective as their presentation of argument in debate. The partnership has endured as much from the freedom they feel in working on independent commissions as from their unity of purpose in working together on others. They accept that they have different talents and skills, and where they are complementary they work together, when not, they support each other with critique and a helping hand. Both see themselves primarily as sculptors who will accept commissions in any medium, but happen at this moment to be working mainly in wood.

It is significant that Mark and Anthony have little specialised training in woodworking. They completed an Art Education course at Melbourne University. Anthony majored in woodcrafts and lectured in this subject for a time, while Mark majored in sculpture and fine arts. After brief careers as art teachers in secondary schools, they went into partnership and began designing and making furniture, which was for them a natural extension of their studies. Their limited knowledge of machine processes and hand skills were initial problems, but they learned rapidly. Their workshop skills have been developed through what they see as artistic expression rather than specific craft activity. They see the purpose of their work as being different to most other craftspersons, as aesthetics alone dominate design decisions, rather than the often-used criteria of convention, precision or 'rightness'.

Woodworkers have a reverence for their medium. Some have an obsession with its colour and figure, fanatically exploiting its qualities. Anthony and Mark consider timber as something to be used only as an element of a total design, having properties of colour and grain which may be an element in the final design: certainly not something to be treated too reverently or allowed to dominate in its effect. They explain, 'At all times we seek to find a balance between the innate beauty of the material we're using and the design we impose upon it. Too many craftsmen allow the material to dominate the design to the point where they depend on the beauty of wood to compensate for poor aesthetic design. We begin work on a design as if we'd never seen a piece of furniture before. Designing a table isn't a matter of using a wood to show off its beautiful qualities, but a unique aesthetic design challenge with certain parameters that require a fresh start every time. Each design has to be a complete philosophical statement if it's to be at all successful.'

While they admire the technical excellence of master craftsmen, they believe this very excellence can be limiting for some and inhibiting for others. 'Creativity requires a balance between technical excellence and conceptual "free-wheeling". However good the past was, that belongs to others. The present and the near future belong to us. The excellence of the past does not demand that we keep repeating it, but to aspire to the same heights of excellence within the limits of our own time and culture. The past should not trap us in a "time-warp" but give us the knowledge and experience to press on, exploring the possibilities presented by the culture and technologies of the present day.'

Whenever the word 'creativity' is mentioned, it induces an electric charge into the conversation. They have worked successfully with creative people, but have found the attitudes of some architects and designers difficult to accept. Mark says, 'It took us a long time to realise that, when working properly, designer-makers are not an appendage to someone else's design process, but independent design professionals who have developed their own area of expertise.' Both Mark and Anthony believe that designer-makers have a significant role to play in both large architectural projects and in the manufacturing industry. 'We, as a professional group, deserve to be recognised as peers of other professional, creative people in our community. Unfortunately, recognition is slow in coming, due in part to some designer-makers who will prototype the designs of others.'

They have had an encouraging response from industry, and have recently undertaken design consultancy work for a number of furniture manufacturers. They don't see themselves as industrial designers, rather as creative designers primarily working on concepts rather than manufacture. Many new materials introduced into the furniture industry, including MDF board, have been used as a timber substitute rather than a timber product having distinctive properties and uses. Anthony believes that the potential of this material has been poorly understood, creating difficulties in the industry. They are often called upon to make modifications to furniture already in production. Anthony sees this as a worthy challenge.

'It's basically easy to come up with a crazy free-wheeling design, but so much more difficult to accept the parameters presented to you by a manufacturer who says, "Modify this to improve the design," but then says with each drawing you present, "You've got to control the design". You are continually reviewing where you are and where the

**Crucifix, rosewood and steel, three-quarters life-size, St Mark's Church, Mt Evelyn, Victoria, Mark Weichard and Anthony Russo.**
Photographer: Anthony Russo.

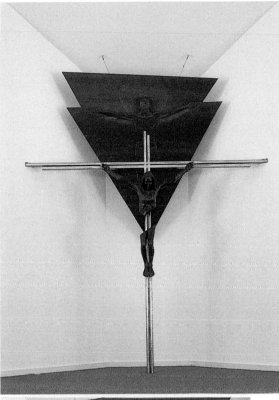

**Crucifix, detail.**
Photographer: Anthony Russo.

115

manufacturer is, in both concept and process, and trying to provide a link. It's an incredibly difficult process to accommodate their technical limitations with a design which satisfies the brief. It makes you appreciate how technology, or the lack of it, determines what can be made. We are so far behind the Italians, who have now moved on to a different phase of technology-based design. They're now exporting the technology rather than the furniture.'

Many designer-makers view industry as an unsympathetic adversary rather than a natural point of contact in woodwork. In Australia, craftspersons have traditionally sought financial support from government-sponsored Arts Council grants. This Anthony and Mark regret: 'We believe that woodworkers have devalued themselves by seeking salvation in grants, not seeing themselves as part of a professional group, and as a

**Pelican in Flight**, Huon pine, blackwood, Perspex and steel, Mark Weichard.
Photographer: Peter Greenwood Brown.

**Female Torso**, rosewood, steel and veneer, Mark Weichard.
Photographer: Shane McLenahan.

Coffee table, silver ash
and rosewood, Anthony
Russo.
Photographer: Anthony
Russo.

**Conference table, Uniquely Australian Corp., Los Angeles, fiddleback ash, myrtle and stainless steel, Anthony Russo.**
Photograph courtesy of Uniquely Australian Corp.

**Credenza table, Uniquely Australian Corp., Los Angeles, burl myrtle, Anthony Russo.**
Photograph courtesy of Uniquely Australian Corp.

consequence accepting reduced expectations and status. Industry has more readily accepted our work than Arts Council administrators. Woodworkers shouldn't expect the support of government funds only, but should seek to promote themselves seriously with industry.'

Although they spend most of their time on corporate and private commissions, an important and increasingly valuable part of their workshop time is devoted to church furniture and carvings. Being rich in ideals and imagery, it enables them to combine sculpture in architectural settings and to experiment with new concepts. They find the freedom in these commissions rewarding, yet are confident that their designs will be appreciated by the congregations. With a rapidly growing population, there is a great demand for three-dimensional religious art in Australia.

Those who review Anthony's furniture have commented on its 'Italian' style. His parents are Italian-born, but he has not visited that country. He disclaims the Italian influence, but admits that the culture has been filtered through from his parents. His work is principally composed of angular planes and sharply splayed edges — in this respect, it is distinctively different to most of his contemporaries. His restrained use of timber as a decorative element on colourful surfaces has won him a number of national awards for corporate and domestic furniture, and its simplicity of line and the balance of masses within the structures have earned him critical acclaim. Anthony has recently received a commission for a huge planar sculpture in concrete and stainless steel for the Pakenham Civic Centre in Melbourne.

Mark's individual works are strongly expressionistic and often best suited to exhibitions. He describes his work: 'Like Gothic religious shrines along the roads of Europe, they contain both image and environment and are meant to provide the "traveller" with a strong insight into life and something to ponder as you stop for a brief moment before them.'

Both Mark and Anthony have exhibited sculpture within the art gallery circuit, and will continue to do so. They believe their work as designer-makers is a natural adjunct to their work as sculptors and directly contributes to their understanding of this field. As they see it, the future of our culture is calling for creative individuals who can position themselves between the two opposing goals of concept and making. Those best able to find this balance will be the ones to create the masterpieces for the next century.

Maintaining both their partnership and professional integrity is a continual contest of will and purpose. Most artists throughout history have only survived with the support of patrons. That has provided conflict of purpose for everyone

**Coffee table, blackwood and ebony, Anthony Russo.**
Photographer: Peter Greenwood Brown.

from Rubens to Rodin. Mark expresses it thus, 'Part of our creative act is to position ourselves beyond the world as it presently exists so we can both maintain our creativity and still return to the professional world, and maintain our finances. The most difficult creative act is to find a balance between your individuality and the demands of a mass culture. Neither extreme can be given in to.' Anthony qualifies this with, '"Art for art's sake" cheapens the fundamentally important relationship between the individual's creativity and the human culture that supports your endeavours. Some part of you has to remain relevant to the world in which you want to be creative by listening to the people you are creating for.'

Without their personal commitment to their art, perhaps those statements could be interpreted as pronouncements of artistic rationalists, but the conviction with which they express them cannot be questioned. A significant problem for anyone who designs for others is achieving that delicate balance between the images your mind creates and your assessment of the brief set by a client. To find the correct aesthetic solution to this puzzle is the task of the successful designer. Orchard Sculpture Design has managed to find that balance with a modicum of self-doubt.

# Side Table

120

**D**esigning for interiors involves special skills. Anthony Russo is often commissioned by clients to make furniture for a particular position and purpose in their home. He is, more than the others featured in this book, an interior designer who specialises in architectural, planar furniture. His side table is characteristic of his work and looks deceptively simple in form. Juxtaposing triangular and rectangular surfaces in a piece of furniture may appear a facile task, but, like architectural interiors, the way they relate to each other in three dimensions determines the success of the design. This commissioned table was designed to stand against a wall and beside steps giving access to a lounge room, its size being prescribed by the narrow space into which it was to fit. It was designed to complement other features in that particular room. Anthony Russo made a small-scale model of the table to confirm the correctness of relationship between the panels and to resolve some of the details for the construction.

Although the table is made from Victorian blackwood, it could be made from any other stable cabinet timber or MDF board. Anthony Russo often uses MDF board in making furniture with a cabinet timber edging as a design feature. If you are substituting MDF board in making this table, you must remember that, although a timber product, MDF has characteristics which should be acknowledged by anyone wishing to use it wisely, and cannot be substituted for timber without those characteristics being considered carefully.

The sliding door conceals a small cabinet, a complication you may wish to avoid. The panel forming this door can be fixed and the back panel omitted if you wish to simplify the construction.

## Making the table

To visualise the components in this table you should first study the exploded drawing, as the workshop drawings can be difficult to interpret. These components are: a top; back frame; a double slab leg; a rail; sliding door (or front panel leg if fixed) and base, shelf and sides for the cabinet. The top and double slab legs are made from panels of Victorian blackwood 28mm thick, while the remaining panels are 25mm thick. These panels are best made from thicknessed

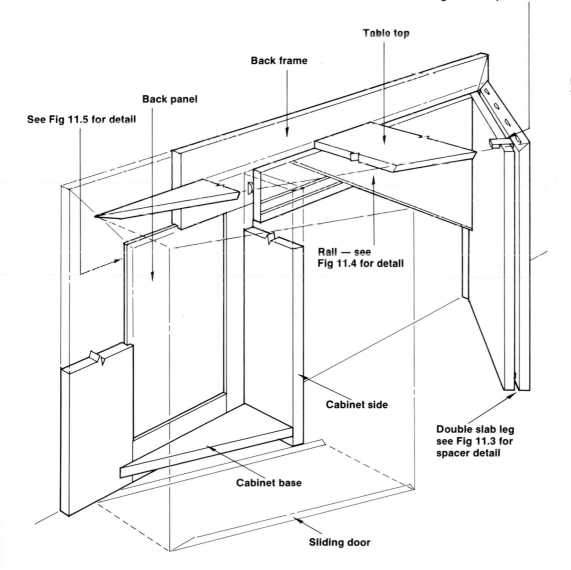

See Fig 11.3 for spacer detail

Table top

Back frame

Back panel

See Fig 11.5 for detail

Fig 11.1 Anatomy of the table.

Rail — see Fig 11.4 for detail

Cabinet side

Double slab leg see Fig 11.3 for spacer detail

Cabinet base

Sliding door

edge-glued boards no wider than 150mm (to avoid cupping).

Anthony used a plate jointer and biscuits in making the edge joints for the panels and in joining most of the members together. This machine simplifies the task of making long mitred or right angle butt joints, but dowels can be used as an alternative method of aligning and strengthening the joints.

## Making the top

● Dress the boards for the top to a thickness of 28mm and cut to lengths of 2000mm. Dress the edges of each board to form gap-free edge joints and align and strengthen the joints with either biscuits or dowels. Glue the panel together and cramp lightly.

● Mark out the shape of the top. Cut the top to shape, retaining the off-cut sections of this panel for later use.

● The 650mm edge will be mitred later to joint to the outer panel of the double slab leg. Plane the long front edge to form a 45° bevel **on the under edge.**

## Making the double slab leg

● Glue up a panel 28mm thick for the double slab leg 1450mm x 660mm, using the method previously described.

● Cut the slabs to lengths of 708mm and 680mm. The 720mm length is to be mitre-jointed to the table top. This joint can be cut with a saw and planed to fit or trimmed using a mitre bit in a router to give an accurate 45° bevel on the end of the outer slab leg and on the 650mm long edge on the table top. Align the joint, using either a plate jointer and biscuits or short dowels.

● Using scrap timber, make two 45° cramping battens 620mm long. Glue these to the surface of the top and slab leg adjacent to the mitre. A strip of thick paper glued between the face of the cramping batten and the face of the blackwood will facilitate the

removal of the batten (*see* Fig 11.2). Clean up the underside of the table top adjacent to the joint and the inside surface of the outer slab leg.

● Glue the joint and cramp lightly with G-cramps. Check the internal faces of the jointer for square, and allow to dry.

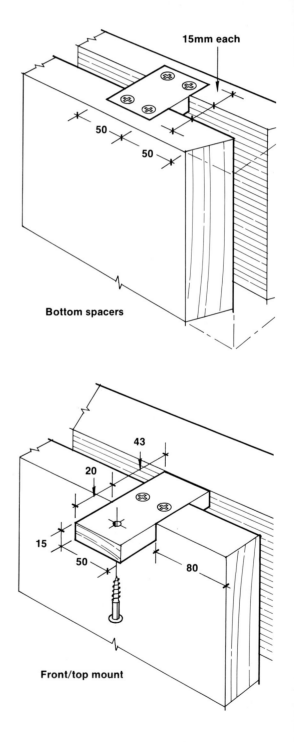

**Bottom spacers**

**Front/top mount**

**Fig 11.2 Outer leg and top joined with 45° mitre, clamping batten with paper between table top and leg, biscuit jointer shown.**

**Fig 11.3 Spacer buttons on the bottom and top edges of the double slab leg.**

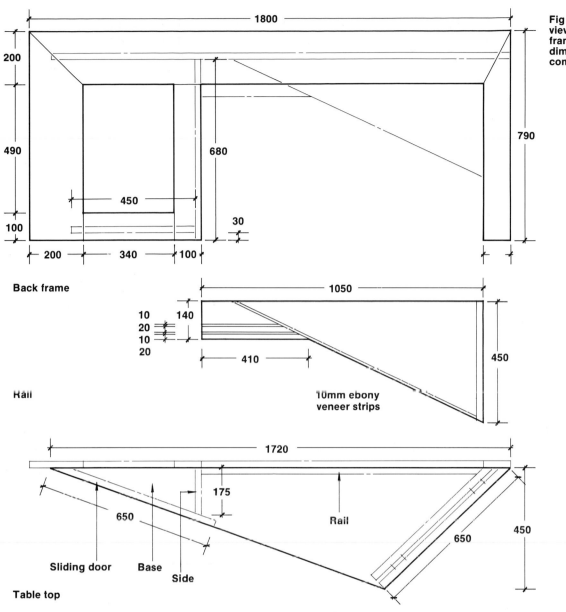

Fig 11.4 Top and front view of the table, back frame and rail, showing dimensions of all components.

**Back frame**

**Rail**

10mm ebony veneer strips

**Table top**

Sliding door    Base    Side    Rail

• The gap between the outer and inner slabs on the leg is 15mm. With the slabs correctly spaced, set out the lap joints for the bottom spacers as shown in Fig 11.3 and cut the joints. Drill for screws and fit the joints.

• Mark and cut the trenches in the top edge of the inner slab to receive the spacer buttons which will secure the inner slab to the underside of the table top and serve as a spacer between the two slabs (see Fig 11.3).

• With the joints dry assembled,

dress the back edges of both slabs flush with the back edge of the table top.

## Making the back panel and cabinet

• Dress the five members of the back panel to sectional size from blackwood 25mm thick and cut them to the length shown in the front view of the table in Fig 11.4. Cut the two mitre joints in the outer members. Using biscuits or dowels to align and strengthen the joints, glue the members together to form the back panel frame.

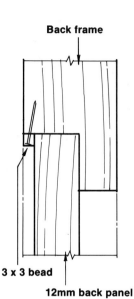

**Fig 11.5 Details of loose back panel.**

Back frame

3 x 3 bead

12mm back panel

• Using a rebate bit in a router, cut a 15mm x 15mm rebate on the rear face and inside edge of the frame, as shown in Fig 11.5.

• Glue up a 12mm thick panel to fit the rebated frame. Trim to size, which will allow a loose-fitting panel in the back frame.

• Prepare a 3mm x 5mm bead to secure the panel.

• Prepare a panel from boards thicknessed to 25mm for the cabinet side. As the panel is to finish 175mm wide, two boards of approximately equal width will be required. Cut the panel to a length of 680mm. Butt-joint this member to the frame, using biscuits or dowels.

• Cut the triangular base for the cabinet from the off-cut material remaining from the top. If the sliding cabinet door is to be fitted, another member of identical size to the cabinet base will be required for a shelf in the cabinet. Butt-joint these members to the cabinet side and the back frame using either biscuits or dowels.

• Sand all surfaces of each member to a fine finish.

• Glue and assemble the cabinet side, base and shelf to the back frame and cramp lightly. When the glue is dry, dress all joints flush and re-sand the dressed faces.

• Apply an ebonising treatment to the back frame, inside face of the cabinet side, base, shelf and inner face of the back panel, and sand very lightly.

## Making the rail

• Using the off-cut material from the table top, mark out the shape of the rail shown in Fig 11.4. Cut to shape and length. Rout trenches in the pattern shown in Fig 11.4, 10mm wide and to a depth which matches the thickness of the veneer to be used as inlay.

• Glue the contrasting veneer to a solid board (Anthony used ebony veneer 0.5mm thick). Paper glued

between the veneer and the board will facilitate the peeling of the veneer from the board. Cut the board into strips exactly the width of the routed trenches and peel the veneer from the board and trim to fit the pattern of trenches. Apply PVA glue to the trench and one face of the inlay, and when dry to the touch, iron the inlay into the trench with an electric iron.

• Trim the rail to length to fit between the cabinet side and the sloping face on the inside of the double slab leg. Note that the top edge of the rail is to fit 60mm below the underside of the table top.

## Assembly, making and fitting the door

• Fix the loose panel in position with the bead.

• Fit plastic button feet to the underside of the outer slab leg, back rail and cabinet side.

• Sand all remaining surfaces to a final finish and apply three coats of Danish oil to all surfaces.

• Glue and screw the inner slab leg to the outer slab leg and the table top with the bottom spacers and the top button spacers.

• The back frame/cabinet assembly is to be screwed to the table top/leg assembly. Drill countersink holes through the back frame for screws and assemble the components by screwing from the back. Fit the rail in position and screw to the back frame, slab leg and cabinet side.

• Prepare a panel for the sliding door from 25mm thick boards, and cut to size 720mm x 650mm. Bevel the upper edge to 45° and bevel the left-hand edge to fit against the face of the back frame. Dress the bevels to ensure the door fits correctly into the face of the cabinet.

• Sand all surfaces of the door and apply three coats of Danish oil.

• Fit the sliding mechanism to the underside of the table top and the

underside of the cabinet base. Fit
the carrier mechanism to the inside
of the door, and adjust the fitting to
allow the door to move freely and
fit with a uniform gap.

● Wax and buff all exposed
surfaces.

**Side table, detail of
cabinet and sliding door.**
Photographer: Peter
Greenwood Brown.

I had read articles Geoff Hague had written on design, but we had not met. I did not know what to expect as I travelled away from the Pacific Highway down a dusty narrow track which skirted farms and wound through heavy timber. Near a cattle yard I came on a battered gate to which was wired a small wooden sign. It said, without explanation, 'Geoff Hague'. The gate was difficult to move, and the car scrambled over a rutted track uphill to a farmhouse, its rusted roof overgrown with wild tobacco and lantana.

Geoff came from the rear door and introduced himself. We talked standing on a rise behind the relic of a house, sheathed in timber boards which were weathered grey, the paint having long departed. Geoff told me it was once home to a family of ten children and was known by the locals as 'Leo's Palace'. I wondered what sad stories this farmhouse could tell of romantic dreams and lost hope, the lot of many who farmed the Australian bush. The whole house is now given over to Geoff's workshop — a saw bench is in the bedroom and a jointer-thicknesser in the kitchen; the back verandah is for hand work, and gluing-up is performed in the lounge.

The isolation and tranquillity are striking, and the workshop can thunder with machinery without annoying anyone. With its modest rent and few distractions, this old farmhouse had much to recommend it as a workshop. To the west lie the temperate rainforests of the Barrington Tops, and down the range are the long sandy beaches of the Myall Lakes National Park, which face the Tasman Sea. Geoff lives with his wife and two small daughters in the coastal community of Tuncurry at the entrance to the Myall Lakes.

His forebears were English master craftsmen who worked as cabinetmakers on Brunel's *SS Great Britain* in the 1840s. At the turn of the century a great-grandfather was a noted furniture maker with a workshop in Digbeth, Birmingham, who worked on the restoration of the medieval woodcarving on Worcester Cathedral. Geoff's own father, an engineer, taught by example as a model-maker, and Geoff recalls making model aircraft using balsa wood — he now sees this as a formative experience in three-dimensional design. Building a model

127

aircraft wing under his father's tutelage was, in his words, 'Like giving a ten-year-old a tertiary education in modern design.'

After attending Goldsmith's College School of Art in London, he set off to see the world and worked throughout Australia for many years, from mining at Mount Isa in the north of Queensland to set design for television. He was a self-employed shop fitter in Sydney when he was offered work as one of the three assistants to Ron Sharp, organ builder for the Concert Hall organ at the Sydney Opera House, a two-year introduction to exceptional musical craftsmanship.

**Geoff Hague collecting spalted tuckeroo with family and friends, Seal Rocks NSW.**
Photographer: Don Finlayson.

After returning from a visit to his parents in England, he settled in Tuncurry to design and make solid timber furniture. He attended a few log auctions, a common event on the north coast, and was introduced to the distinctive qualities of rosewood, rose she-oak, red mahogany, and in turn to Tasmanian myrtle, blackwood and Huon pine, becoming an enthusiast for fine native timbers.

For him, these timbers have a distinctive colour palette unlike those he had used in the UK. He feels that colour contributes significantly to the character of a piece, either subduing its effect or, as in the case of his orchid stool which uses the uncommon socket sassafras, making the piece even truer with its acid yellow colouring.

The sculptor shows in his work, and the Fine Arts study in our discussions on design. Here I encountered a craftsman whose vocabulary and knowledge were unlike those of others with whom I had debated this subject. To talk as we did in that kitchen, with bird and butterfly books on the mantlepiece, about the influence of the Moors and Gothic master craftsmen from France on the furniture of Spain in the Middle Ages, was not what I expected. That afternoon we ranged over centuries of European culture and tried to make sense of its influence on a startlingly new, polyglot society like Australia, transposed in time and physical isolation to a landscape unlike that of any other country on earth. We searched for influences and emphases, identified fashion and authentic craft, and parted with the issues somewhat resolved. At least we came to the conclusion that to follow what Geoff Hague calls 'ubiquitous magazine fashion' in furniture design is a mistake, if only because, as he says, 'it distracts everyone from looking at those things right in front of them that possess all the vocabulary of design you'd ever need for a lifetime's work.' The real delight, as he sees it, of being here in Australia is that it is all there waiting to be done.

He sees the visual languages of the flora and fauna as the source for his notions on design. 'I returned to England and realised how urbanised and domesticated life there is. The landscape is rendered almost entirely for human use, and ends up being, in a sad way, loved to death. I suspect that's why I've made my home in Australia. Here there isn't the same preoccupation with the past that engenders a basic conservatism and reliance on tradition, or conversely, a tyranny that demands an overreaction that is jarringly aggressive and seems to be not particularly interested in beauty. I much prefer to create at will, without this need for overreaction. In many European countries it just isn't possible to work as a cabinetmaker unless you have formal training. I can't think of anything more inhibiting than being told you musn't create without training — that the ''excited effort'' in making a piece isn't enough.'

He sees clients as an exciting source of ideas, as they frequently commission pieces that he would not necessarily

**Native orchid stool, socket sassafras.**
Photographer: Michael Gill.

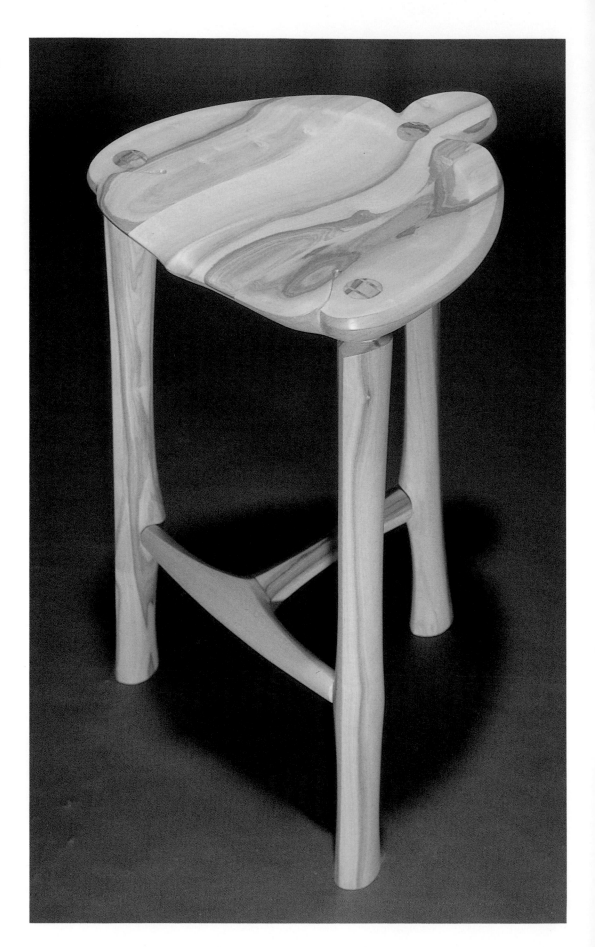

have considered. The north coast of New South Wales is a veritable treasure-trove of cabinet timbers, and most of the older residents have a cache of valuable timber retrieved from isolated valleys. His current commission is for a Catholic chapel at Port Macquarie: the silky oak for the lectern, altar and presidential chair has been supplied by the church, and had been lovingly stored away in their workshop for the past eight years or more.

His own designs are signature pieces. The stool, chair and wine table have developed gradually over the past three years, and he now makes variations that keep the workshop operating between commissions. He finds that the initial concrete idea is sound but often inadequate in its details, and it takes time to see these inadequacies, which are then improved gradually by trial and error. He expressed this as 'developing a sensibility which is classical and metaphorical rather than eclectic and representational'.

We spoke of the place of furniture in the last decade of the 20th century and how, with the forthcoming revolution in technology, anyone making hand-made items can seem irrelevant. To provide a sense of balance, he spoke of how his wife's sister, after marrying her Balinese fiancé, returned after the wedding ceremony in Bali with wedding presents for his wife and children all made by members of the groom's family: a large ceremonial fan, camphorwood carvings and a balsawood model horse for the children. He felt reassured that the people of a small tropical island had the unselfconscious faith in their own ability to make things of beauty for everyday use.

To add another dimension to his woodworking, he recently began teaching handicapped adults basic woodwork skills. 'To spend the day in the workshop trying to do the very best I can do and then spend the next teaching an intellectually handicapped person to do the very best they can do is a very sobering experience, and almost guarantees you don't become too conceited about what you are achieving.'

We form images in our mind of those who write as we read their words. I expected an erudite intellectual in Geoff Hague, for his words are structured and his arguments learned. I found to my surprise a liberated soul who has found a means of sculpting in furniture with a wonderfully expressive sense, yet someone who has come to this achievement though study and a knowledge of matter rather than acquired skills. What does this tell us about the professional growth of a successful woodworker? There certainly is no one lone path to creative expression in any medium — we all grow professionally at our own rate, following whichever path suits our temperament, abilities and past experience. Geoff Hague has intuitively plotted that path with a resolve which has ensured his success.

*Map of the World*
**jewellery box, Huon pine and spalted tuckeroo.**
Photographer: Michael Gill.

# Tuckeroo Breakfast Chair

**T**his chair has been variously called a Chinese chair and a breakfast chair, with the facetious name 'tuckeroo', having a significance which only Australians would appreciate. It is a sitting chair ideal for casual living, being light yet robust and comfortable. As the members are laminated it can be made from light cabinet timbers, even though all the members are slender and curved.

Geoff Hague first designed this chair without a backrest, which simplified the design and its manufacture, but the back rail, set low, caught the lower back of the sitter. The curve on the back rail was modified, and a shaped backrest added. The 10mm thick intarsia inlay on this backrest is of a spalted rainforest species in a contrasting colour. Many minor modifications have been made to the design, but the structure of the chair has not altered since it was first designed in 1988.

## Making the chair

Although unconventional in using a base frame on the floor, the chair has members similar in purpose to those found in conventional chairs. The arms and back rail form an upper assembly which is replicated at floor level with a similar frame. The base side rails are identical in shape to the arms. The seat is shaped from solid timber, and to allow for expansion and contraction the seat rails are placed close together and fixed

to the seat with sliding dovetails. The seat rails are dovetailed to the front rail and are jointed to the back legs with mortice and tenons.

Any quality cabinet timber could be used to make this chair, but select a timber for the seat which is suitable for hand carving. If the intention is for the laminations to be inconspicuous, the components to be laminated should be cut from consecutive boards or the timber carefully chosen to ensure that grain and colour match.

To assist in accurately setting out the joints, a working rod of the side view of the chair should be made on a sheet of plywood. To ensure that the top and bottom frames are also the correct shapes and sizes when assembled, working rods of the top and base frames should be made showing all the joints. It is not necessary to show the shape of each member, only the position of each joint relative to the others.

**Tuckeroo breakfast chair, blackwood, jacaranda and spalted tuckeroo.**
© Geoff Hague.
Photographer: Michael Gill.

**Detail of tuckeroo breakfast chair.**
Photographer: Michael Gill.

GEOFF HAGUE • TUCKEROO BREAKFAST CHAIR

**Fig 12.1 Anatomy of the tuckeroo breakfast chair.**

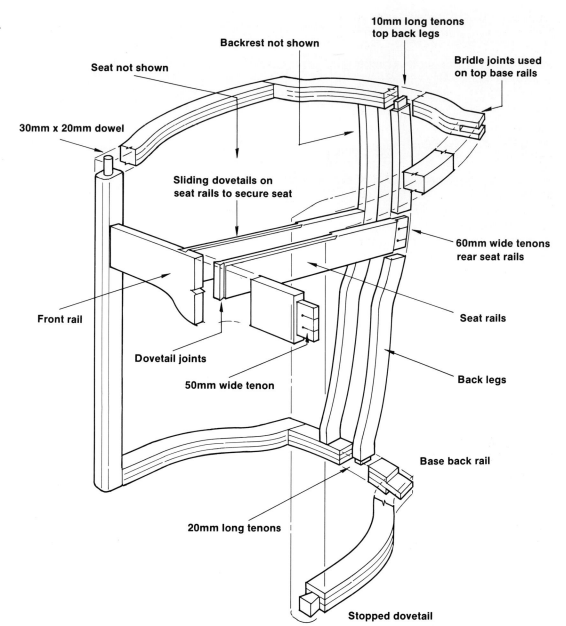

10mm long tenons
top back legs

Backrest not shown

Bridle joints used
on top base rails

Seat not shown

30mm x 20mm dowel

Sliding dovetails on
seat rails to secure seat

60mm wide tenons
rear seat rails

Front rail

Seat rails

Dovetail joints

50mm wide tenon

Back legs

Base back rail

20mm long tenons

Stopped dovetail

## Making the top and base frames

● Make full-size drawings of the templates on plywood. Note that the joints and 5mm waste have been allowed for on the templates, as shown in Fig 12.2.

● Cut out the templates, leaving sufficient waste to allow the edges to be dressed to give smooth, continuous curves.

● Thickness the timber required for the laminates in each member to 10mm. Careful thicknessing will simplify the construction of the

bridle joints in each frame.

● Cut the boards required for the laminates to width and length. Sizes are shown on the template drawings. The following number of laminates will be required: three back rails, twelve arms and base side rails and three base rails. (These members can be identified in Fig 12.1.)

● Trace out the shape of each laminate from the template and cut to shape, leaving at least 1mm waste to be trimmed.

● Secure the template to each

laminate with double-sided tape or by pinning the template with fine brads to a face of the laminate which will not be visible when the laminates are glued. Using a trimming bit (46/95) in a router, dress the edges of each laminate. This will ensure that matching laminates are identical in shape, and simplify gluing.

• To simplify the making of the bridle joints at the corner of each frame, trim to length a centre laminate for each arm and base side rail to form the peg section of the bridle joint. Leave 2mm waste to be chiselled later when fitting the joint. Similarly trim to length the outside laminates for the back rail and base rail to form the tenon section of the bridle joints, leaving 2mm waste to be removed later to form the shoulders of the joint. These laminates should be marked to length from the working rods for the top and base frames.

• Glue the laminates together in sets of three to form the two arms, two base side rails, back rail and base rail. Cramp the laminates lightly with G-cramps and allow the glue to dry.

• Trim the bridle joints to fit, and assemble the frames. Check the alignment of the joints by placing the assembled frame over the working rods.

• Glue each joint separately and, after checking for alignment on the working rod, clamp lightly with a G-cramp, allowing each joint to dry before gluing the next joint in the frame.

• Remove the waste from each bridle joint and dress all edges and faces.

## Making the front legs

• Prepare the timber for the legs to sectional size 40mm x 35mm and cut to a length of 580mm.

• Turn the 40mm x 20mm diameter dowel on the end of each leg. Mark the angled shoulder on the dowel

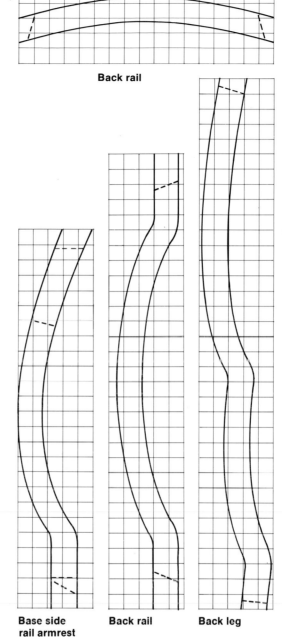

**Fig 12.2 Templates drawn on 20mm grid.**

Back rail

Base side rail armrest    Back rail    Back leg

from the working rod and cut the shoulder. Mark the finished length of the leg from the working rod.

• Bore a 20mm diameter hole in the arms to match the dowel. Mark the centre for the holes from the working rod, noting that the hole is bored at an angle to the face of the arm.

• Set out the stopped dovetail joint between the bottom of the leg and the base frame. Note when setting out the dovetail that the leg is to be shaped as shown in Fig 12.3, and that the dovetail, if made too large, will weaken the joint. Cut the joint and fit.

• Set out the position of the mortice for the front rail, and chop the mortice.

• Shape the leg to the cross section shown in Fig 12.3.

## Making the front and seat rails

• Prepare the front rail to sectional size 90mm x 20mm and cut to a length of 525mm. Shape the rail as shown in the front view of Fig 12.3.

• Mark out the tenon joints, marking the distance between shoulders from the working rod. Cut the joint.

**Fig 12.3 Dimensions and structural details of the tuckeroo chair.**

• Prepare the seat rails to sectional size 60mm x 20mm and cut to a length of 465mm.

• Mark out the angled shoulders of the dovetail and the tenon joints on either ends from the working rod. Set out the position of the dovetails on the front rail, as shown in Fig 12.3, and cut both joints.

## Making the back legs

• Cut the 10mm boards previously thicknessed for laminates to width and length for the back legs. (Note that only two laminates are required for each leg.) Cut and shape as previously described for other shaped members.

• Set out the mortice and tenons on either end of the back legs,

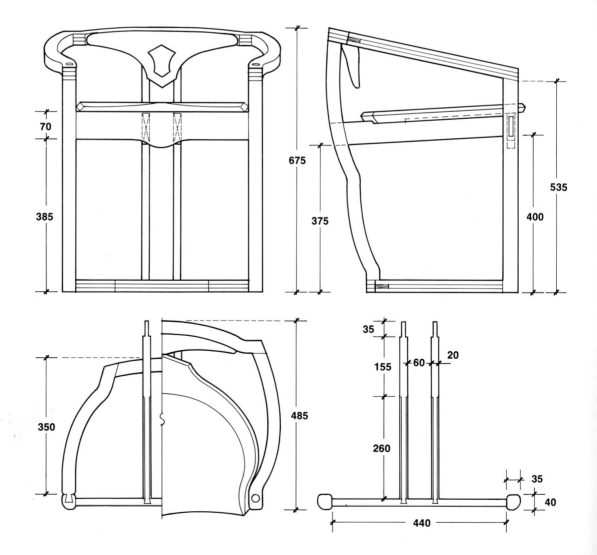

marking the shoulders of the tenons from the working rod. Cut the joints.

• Set out the mortice on each back leg from the working rod, to match the tenons on the seat rails. Chop the mortices.

## Making the seat

• Thickness the timber to 35mm for the seat and cut lengths of 450mm. To reduce cupping, each board should not exceed 150mm in width. Sufficient boards will be required to give a total width of 520mm when edge-glued. After the glue has dried, plane one face flat.

• Mark out the shape of the seat from the template shown in Fig 12.4 and the sliding dovetails on the underside of the seat as shown in Fig 12.5. These joints can be cut using a dovetailing bit in a router. Note that the dovetail grooves change to rectangular grooves at the back of the seat.

• Set out and cut the 45mm wide rebate on the front edge of the seat as shown in Fig 12.5.

• Cut the seat to shape and form the splay on the top edges and round the under edges with a spokeshave and block plane. Carve the shape to the top surface of the seat with a No. 7 gouge and sand the surface.

## Making the backrest

• Mark the backrest to shape from the template shown in Fig 12.6 on 50mm thick timber, and cut to shape.

• The curve on the back face of the backrest is shaped to fit the curve on the front edge of the back rail. This curve can be marked from the back rail, cut with a bandsaw and finally shaped to a matching gap-free fit with a plane. The outer edges of the backrest are also shaped to be comfortable when sitting in the chair.

• Cut out the 10mm thick intarsia inlay and rout the shape in the

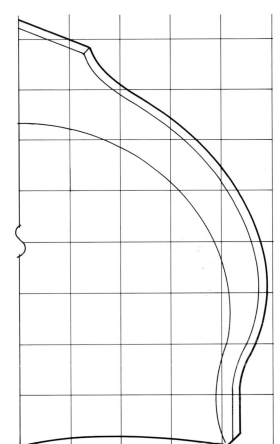

**Fig 12.4 Half shape of seat drawn on 50mm grid.**

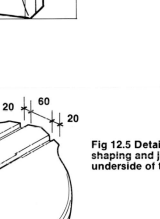

**Fig 12.5 Details of shaping and joints on the underside of the seat.**

**Fig 12.6 Shape of backrest drawn on 20mm grid.**

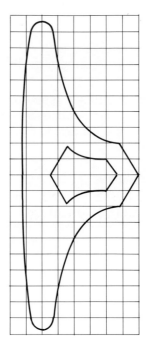

**Prototype of Chinese breakfast chair.
© Geoff Hague.**
Photographer: Michael Gill.

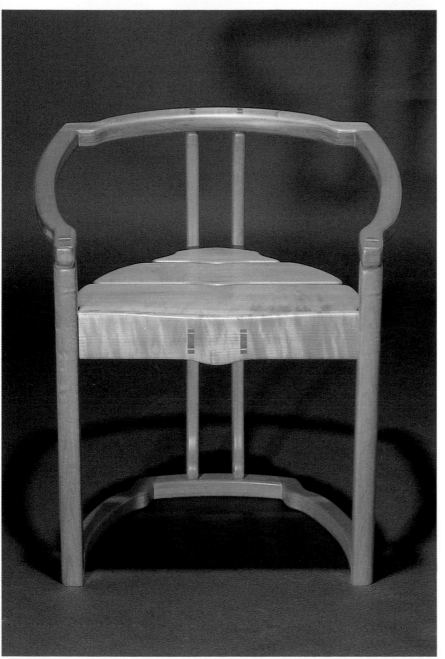

backrest. Fit, glue and cramp lightly. When dry, dress the inlay flush with the face of the backrest.

• The backrest is glued and screwed to the back rail, the screws entering from the underside of the back rail.

## Assembly and finishing

• Make a trial assembly of the chair and a final fitting of all joints.

• Round over the arrises on the shoulders of the joints at either end of the front and back legs.

• Sand all surfaces with ascending grades of 120, 180 and 240 grit abrasive paper.

• Glue the front rail to the two front legs. Wedge the tenons, using wedges made from the same timber as used in the seat. Cramp lightly, check for square and allow to dry. Dress off waste from the tenons.

• Glue the remainder of the members, cramp lightly and allow to dry.

• Dress off waste from all remaining joints and sand to a finished surface.

• Geoff Hague finished the chair by applying two coats of fine buffing oil, and buffed the surfaces by hand.

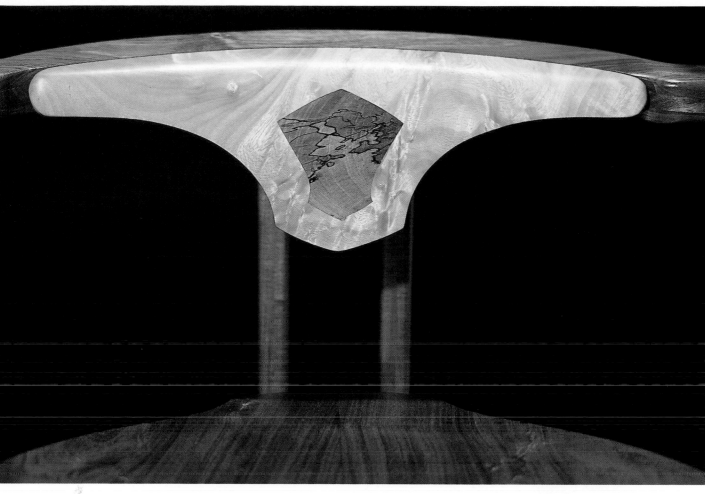

**Detail of tuckeroo breakfast chair.**
Photographer: Michael Gill.

**Gay Hawkes in the horizontal scrub.**
Photographer: Q Photographics.

creates imaginative sculptures which are also chairs, altars, cupboards and furniture. Both these artists have an expressive song to sing about their homeland, the life of its people and the beauty of its landscape. Both have chosen to express this in furniture and sculptured wood through disparate processes, and each has a great admiration for the other's work.

Many who have made a study of Australian furniture consider the work of Gay Hawkes to represent that which is quintessentially Australian. Others place her work alongside that of leading contemporary sculptors. It is, however, self-defeating to attempt to classify her work, which is as brilliant as wooden furniture as it is as sculpture. Where one appreciation begins and the other ceases is a pointless exercise in tautology. Although in this book we will be considering it as furniture, to save duality of description, it is what the reader believes it to be. You should make your judgement after considering what it is that Gay Hawkes is endeavouring to say through her work.

Most woodworkers have their timber delivered. Gay Hawkes leaves her workshop in inner-city Melbourne and drives her utility truck to the Arve Valley in the south-west of Tasmania, via the Bass Strait ferry, to collect her timber supply. Where better to re-energise the spirit, the source and inspiration for her work, than to live for a time in the place she loves and from which she can collect the wood she works with? Horizontal scrub grows as a dense tangled mass on the forest floor in this part of Tasmania. Often it is difficult to cut unless the forest has been disturbed by bulldozers used for logging. It is so dense that machine operators have been known to fall with their bulldozers through layers of horizontal scrub which had obliterated gullies. This dense, hard wood has a bark which remains permanently attached. Durable and extremely strong, it forms the frame of many of Gay Hawkes' constructions. She also collects 'feral' woods and driftwood, from which she gains inspiration and joy. To listen to her describe that process of *discovery* — eyes wide, hands moving expressively to define the piece, and voice evocative — is to appreciate the magic of that inspiration. That place and that time is very important to her work — it is the time of inspiration, the time when Gay Hawkes lives a special creative experience that provides the power and meaning for her work.

Like most of the craftsmen represented here, Gay came to her vocation relatively late in life. She was living outside Hobart on a small farm, and accepted a job as an arts liaison officer in the city. To promote the community centre, she began designing posters. This led to her enrolling in an Associate Diploma in Design at the Hobart School of Art, with the intention of studying printmaking. She admits, 'I wasn't very good at printmaking as I work better in three dimensions, and when Kevin Perkins, who was a lecturer in wood design, gave me a wooden spoon to carve, I was away. At first no one at the school appreciated what I was trying to do. I'd never worked with tools before, and wanted to work with green timber. Even Kevin told me it couldn't be done, but I didn't have that past training in cabinetmaking. I made a chair, and I can still remember splitting peppermint gum for the seat with an axe, shaping it with a bowsaw and boring the holes with a brace and bit. I did all the final shaping with a drawknife. My work took off like a bush fire — I became obsessed. Shortly after, I was asked to exhibit in Adelaide at the Festival Centre Gallery. The response was a great surprise, but since then I haven't worried how I would sell my work or where. I make it for myself. If others appreciate it, that's good, but it doesn't worry me if people don't understand what I'm trying to say.

'In 1982 Kevin Perkins encouraged me to apply for an Australia Council Grant. Prior to that I worked at the University for a year to get some tools together, build a workshop and feed my three children. During that year I worked late at night on furniture and constructed an innovative tent workshop in my backyard. Most people don't understand the conviction I have for each piece I make. Once I have an idea, I'd go mad if I couldn't make it. It's not as if I can put a piece aside for a month or two and return to work at it slowly. Once I start, I'm compelled to make it. When I'm working at my hut in Tasmania and I have an idea, I literally run, collecting pieces of driftwood or timber to work with. Quite often a chair could be made in a matter of a few hours. Part of the inspiration comes from the pieces themselves — one piece of driftwood might suggest an arm, the curve on another the back of the chair. I also read and write a great deal. Writing usually takes up the first few hours of each day, my journal or letters to friends. I have always been interested in politics, and many of my pieces have a social or political message. I even carve words on the seat or back of some pieces. I tend to design by writing and drawings together, as words are very important to me.'

Although the isolation and loneliness of Tasmania have a great impact on her work, she admits that she needs the urban environment of Melbourne to provide a balance. As she walks at a brisk pace through the busy streets of Melbourne, she seems to be at home there as well. It is the people who provide that other part of her inspiration, and she enters into the life of the urban community with the same vitality with which she works in Tasmania. Two greater extremes in lifestyle would be difficult to find, but they obviously complement each other perfectly. Gay Hawkes' workshop is in what were stables at the rear of an old factory in a quiet backstreet, an ideal if cluttered space in which to work. A bench sits beneath the window, a

**Anzac Figures and Crucifix.**

woodstove in one corner, and a scattering of finished pieces and some timber fill the space. A portable power drill and bandsaw are the only visible machines, and drawknives and a few chisels hang on a board. Compared with other workshops it is fundamental, but what else could Gay Hawkes use? On a rough brick wall at the rear of the workshop hang a number of small crucifixes made from shaped brush timber. The face of each figure is carved, but the natural forms of the timber suggest outstretched hands and splayed legs, gaunt and gnarled. Strangely, there is not an expression of agony in any of them,

**The Trembling Stranger chair.**
Photographer:
Q Photographics.

which is more easily understood when Gay explains that they are not necessarily intended to have the usual religious significance.

'I was brought up as a Baptist, the sixth generation of Irish emigrants, and taught the scriptures by my parents. That's given my life a richness and knowledge I've valued and explains why I'm interested in these symbols of our culture. I can take those things I've learnt as a child which I value and discard those things my intellect tells me are questionable. I suppose I carve crucifixes because I'm fascinated by this symbol of martyrdom on the cross. It's the martydom that I'm trying to depict, Jesus Christ, women, political prisoners and prisoners of conscience. Death for a cause is the ultimate in human endeavour, yet also the ultimate in foolishness — complete madness. At the time of the hunger strikes in Ireland I made a chair as a salute to Bobby Sands. The figures hanging there come directly from my subconscious. I was imbued with the power of the crucifixion as a child, and I try to capture some of that agony, like Mantegna did in his paintings. I've made six crucifixes now, and none look agonised, they look patient or serene or even comical in some way. I find it interesting that my intention is rarely able to be translated into an agonised expression. Something must dictate that it doesn't come out that way.'

Standing out from the wall of her workshop is a large piece which looks like a horse, front hoof raised, neck strongly arched. On the back is the gaunt figure of a rider, probably a man. Gay explains, 'That piece is a cupboard,' and opens a door on the back of the horse in explanation. 'It depicts the Australian legend of the drover. It's not just an historical figure of the drover and his wife — the woman is still to be built — but it's something of what I know about Australian men and women, the way they relate to each other now and then, in time. The sculptures are furniture, and both pieces will be cabinets. They're meant to be used in a house, not displayed in a gallery.' The strength of that tall horse, as Gay pulls it across the floor on its three earthbound feet, suggests that her skill at joining pieces, if not jointing, produces greater structural integrity than found in many conventional pieces of furniture.

Whether those fortunate people who own one of Gay Hawkes' 'creations' bought it for its sculptural qualities or as furniture is immaterial. That they appreciated the unique quality of her genius is undoubtedly part of their reason for wanting to own a tangible expression of a very independent Australian spirit. It is simple to write about the cultural and physical qualities of this country, but difficult to encapsulate something which is quintessentially Australian. Gay Hawkes, in spirit and product, comes closest to its true representation.

**Detail, *The Trembling Stranger*.**
Photographer: Q Photographics.

**Detail of seat, *The Trembling Stranger*.**
Photographer: Q Photographics.

# Anzac Chair

**A**ll the other project designs in this book can be made by following the instructions and reading the drawings. Perhaps some will need modifying to suit your workshop or the timber you may acquire. **There is no intention, however, that you will ever make an Anzac chair.** Hopefully, after you read this and reflect on what Gay Hawkes has done, you too may wish to make a chair which is inspired by events in your day, with timber you have found. It looks deceptively simple, but the challenge is not just to make something which looks like a chair. Rather it is to express yourself by sculpting something on which to sit.

Many have classified Gay Hawkes' work as 'bush furniture', meaning that it is made from unmilled timber in a rudimentary manner. This classification is arbitrary when the true nature of her work is examined. Gay's early work was inspired by the Tasmanian 'Jimmy Possum' chair and Irish country chairs, typical of County Leitrim. These fundamental Irish chairs were made by boring holes in a split board which formed the seat, into which were fitted legs and back spindles made from found branches. They proved not only robust, but had an honesty and structural simplicity which was later formalised and reproduced using machined timber. No doubt the first chairmakers in High Wycombe were similarly inspired by country chairs from southern England.

Since those early days of chairmaking we have been schooled in the appreciation and manufacture of furniture with machined

members in designs intended for mass-production. Our eye is attuned to the mechanical, and usually we judge the quality of a piece by its trueness and the precision of its construction and finish. It is difficult for us to remember that this was not always so, and that a chair or box was once judged solely on the merits of its fitness for purpose and structural integrity. This is not to suggest that we have become corrupted in our refinement, but it is possible that we view furniture with an eye jaundiced by the rightness and trueness of everything in our made environment. An Irish country chair would have looked appropriate in an 18th-century home in Ballyporeen, with its roughly rendered walls and with lintels and roof beams made from found timbers. We must make considerable mental adjustments, however, when we view that same chair in the 'right' environment of a museum.

Perhaps we have lost something with our technological mastery of timber. Any member in a chair can now be shaped to a designer's whim, irrespective of the complexity of grain or hardness of the timber being used. The Irish peasant made his design choice when he picked up a branch to use as a leg in his home-crafted chair. He had no need to sketch the profile of that leg. The shape was a matter of selection, not the result of a process. It is best not to forget, however, that the peasant was a designer-maker, with a creative integrity possibly missing in many woodworkers of today.

How you begin making a chair with found

**Anzac chair.**
© **Gay Hawkes.**
Photographer: Evan Clark.

146

**Gay Hawkes cutting
horizontal scrub.**
Photographer:
Q Photographics.

material will depend on your experience in working with this material and your understanding of the nature of self-expression. The technique used by Gay Hawkes is her personal approach to creating furniture and, while possibly not unique, needs careful explanation. By reading passages from her journal, we can trace the thoughts and emotions which inspired the Anzac chair. From these you can assess that it would not be possible for you to emulate that procedure — however, it may inspire you to create something from found materials, or it may cause you to reflect on the process you use to design and the origin of the mental images which give it form.

No description is provided of the jointing process used by Gay Hawkes in making the Anzac chair. Each joint is a unique design problem created by the shape and size of the material selected for each member. Conventional and unconventional solutions may be found for each problem. Gay Hawkes uses a bowsaw for shaping and cutting, portable power drill for boring holes in very brittle wood, and a drawknife and chisel to shape the surfaces for jointing. Where possible the joint is a mortice and tenon, usually wedged, and glued if the timber is seasoned. Dowels and nails can also be used if the face of the timber will accept these. The decision where each can be used is your decision, and experience alone will determine which is the most appropriate. Remember that you are creating a structure which must be rigid and sound. If you find creating innovative structures difficult, it may be best to study conventional furniture and look at how it has been strengthened with rungs and binding members.

The word 'Anzac' is an anagram developed during World War I to identify members of the Australian and New Zealand Army Corps. The Anzac legend was written in the disastrous Gallipoli campaign of 1915, when Australian, New Zealand and British troops attempted to capture the Gallipoli Peninsula, planning to gain control of the Dardanelles and access to the Black Sea. The Anzacs landed on 25 April, and withdrew after suffering horrendous casualties on 9 January, 1916. Few countries commemorative a military disaster with a national holiday, but in Australia 25 April, Anzac Day, is a peculiar day of mixed emotions for most Australians: of sadness at the futility of war, yet pride in their nation. In many respects it has become Australia's national day, the equivalent of St David's Day for Wales or Independence Day for the USA. The Anzac legend of comradeship and sacrifice is an important part of the Australian psyche.

To commemorate the 75th anniversary

of the Gallipoli landing, 46 veterans of that campaign were flown by the Australian Government to Turkey. Anzac Day 1990 saw them attend a dawn service on the cliffs overlooking the beaches where they had landed in 1915. That service was televised live in Australia and broadcast over national radio. It was a moving and memorable event, which for confused reasons still brings tears to my eyes. We followed the departure of those old veterans from Australia, their arrival in Turkey and progress back to Gallipoli nightly on radio or television.

Gay Hawkes had arrived in Tasmania on a timber-collecting excursion on 2 April of that year, and listened to the nightly bulletins leading up to the departure of the veterans for Gallipoli. She wrote in her journal on that day:

'There comes a time when one must choose between contemplation and action . . . for a proud heart there can be no compromise. There is God or Time, that cross or his sword . . .'

Camus, The Absurd Man

Then on 20 April the entry:

'I am washed up in a flood of memories and anecdotes about the Anzacs, the myths of Australia. I want to create this martyrdom and also some sort of Resurrection, for without the one we cannot have the other.'

Then a break until 25 April:

'On Anzac Day 1990, rose at 5 a.m. and drove into Hobart, but missed the Dawn Service — day broke as I crossed to Midway Point — beautiful reflections. Then to the Huon [valley], mists and blue satin river with reflections . . . In the Arve [valley] I couldn't even force my way into Creek [through the horizontal scrub] so went on to the Loop . . . — cut for hours and loaded up by 3 p.m. So many bees and leatherwood blooming. I drove back to Franklin Tavern — there even H was drunk, and the ex-convicts in the bar all foul and loud. But it was good and the whole day perfect. Especially

returning over the mountains to Ferntree as mist and rain wreathed the slopes right through to the sea.

'Now 27.4.90 — back at the B'house. So wet, much cooler and trying to do some work . . .

'Yesterday at Franklin I was stopped in my tracks by a sudden vivid colour — wreaths and flowers placed at the foot of a marble soldier, standing in the evening light on the very edge of the river — a sight so simple, so pagan — the offering so FINE. I stood transfixed and then crossed the road for a whiskey!

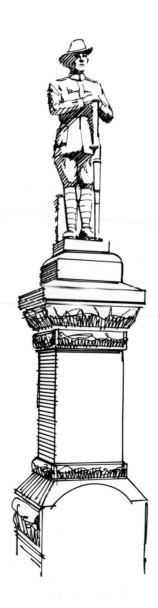

War Memorial at Franklin, Tasmania.

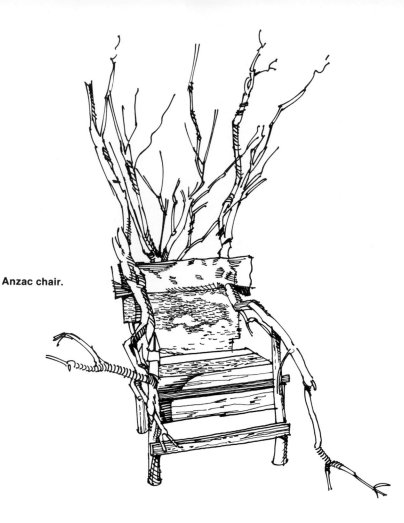

**Anzac chair.**

**Details of Anzac chair.**
Photographer: Evan
Clark.

'LATER — When I made my Anzac chair I placed it under the she-oaks, like a shrine. After my trip to Lagoon Bay, collecting wood, whalebones and mushrooms, I put two dishes of mushrooms on the seat — pink, grey, brown and white like the driftwood — my oblation to the Gods which provide the riches of this place . . .

'''Blessed, Blessed be the vine-knife! What has become perfect, everything ripe – wants to die''
                Nietzsche, Eternal Recurrance

'. . . May call the chair "S E Tasmania ANZAC DAY 1990".'

At this time Gay Hawkes also sculpted from her firewood a set of 'Anzac figures' of the gaunt, resolute 'diggers' who returned to Gallipoli. They are set on a tiered cupboard depicting the cliffs of Anzac Cove set beneath a crucifix.

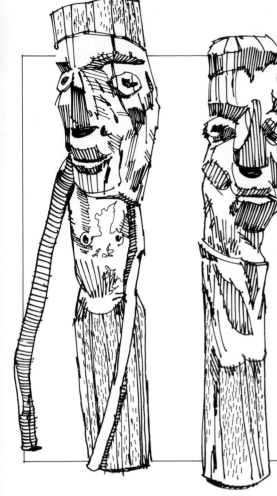

**Anzac figures carved
from firewood.**

**Details of Anzac figures.**
Photographer: Evan
Clark.

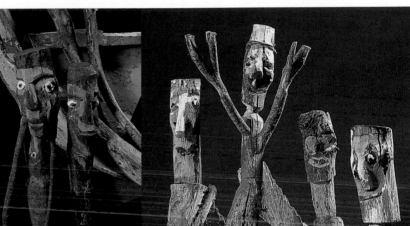

On 28 April she wrote:

"". . . heroism, patriotism, sacrifice,
courage undaunted. Youth and now age
and a new country exploring its identity
in foreign parts . . .""

Jeg Møter Fortelle

""You have migrated with raging soul far
from the paternal home, passing beyond
the seal's double rocks, and you now
inhabit a foreign land.""

Medea'

Few who work in wood find their
inspiration, as Gay Hawkes does, from a
combination of nature, reading, writing and
philosophising. Many share her profound
love of nature and could appreciate her
supreme dedication, but few create in wood
with her untrammelled vision and
intellectual rigour. Be inspired by her
creativity to attempt a chair in found
materials which says what *you* want it to say.

**Anzac figures in the
prow of a boat.**
Photographer: Evan
Clark.

151

At some time in their life, everyone experiences an event which affects them so profoundly that they feel compelled to reflect on the nature of the experience and ask fundamental questions about their personal values or beliefs. That chance viewing of Leon Sadubin's refectory table in 1978 was such an experience for me: it was not initially inspirational in a creative sense, but by awakening an interest in furniture design it caused me to review my attitudes to the relationship between interiors and lifestyle.

Leon Sadubin's name is synonymous with fine woodwork in Australia. Like Kevin Perkins, his name calls up images of grace and beauty in furniture. Both have different signatures in their craft, but share a common sympathy for the colour and figure in timber which is unmatched in this country. Both have the quiet manner of craftsmen who are supremely confident of their creative expression, and the natural charm of those who have no need for pretence.

It says something for the place of designer-makers in Australia that few people have heard of their names, although both feature often in craft magazines and their work is known amongst those who work in wood or who appreciate finely crafted furniture. Why are designers in Australia not given the public respect of those in Scandinavia or Italy? Why are their names and faces not well known? Perhaps Leon and Kevin would not want this, but, in terms of their contribution to the Australian ethos, it is their due.

Leon Sadubin's workshop is on a busy arterial road in a northern suburb of Sydney. Traffic flows past all day, and conversation in his showroom is punctuated by the roar of trucks. You enter through a sliding door made from silky oak and shaped like a bowsaw. His sign advertising 'Wood Works' swings above the wide verandah which fronts the street. Of late his showroom has given way to a woodworking tool- and bookstore, but his original writing desk stands at one end complementing an unusually shaped dining table and chairs. The bookshelves and display cases lining the walls are as beautifully detailed and precisely made as any of his furniture. That is the mark of Leon Sadubin's true professionalism, an attention to the most minute detail relating to his work and its presentation. His promotion is a natural extension of the man himself, not a constructed image.

Behind the showroom is a well-ordered workshop. Below in the basement is the heavy-duty machinery capable of handling the large quantities of Australian hardwoods which pass through them. There is little evidence of dust and disorder, the trademarks of most woodworkers. Rather, there is a neatness and order which made me reflect on where he has stored that clutter of inspirations yet to be finalised in a product, so common in most workshops.

**Leg and end detail of a refectory table.**
Photographer: Scott Donkin.

I felt relaxed sitting on one of Leon's comfortable chairs, talking to him about Australian design. His contribution to the conversation, as I have grown to expect, was well reasoned. Leon has a habit of smiling often and frowning seldom, as he seems at peace with himself. He 'knows what he's about', and although the conversation was on a subject he has addressed often in public, his argument seems fresh and was expressed with confidence and enthusiasm.

When he resigned from teaching 14 years ago, he was quite certain of his future direction. His first commissions were made in a home workshop, and in 1977 Leon and his wife Ginny acquired a small workshop at Thornleigh. He began working with an assistant, making domestic furniture while Ginny developed her own range of Australian souvenirs made from off-cuts. In 1982 Leon was awarded a Churchill Fellowship, which allowed him to study small workshop organisation in Denmark and to learn woodcarving with a master carver, Peter Wirschig, in West Germany. He admired the balance achieved in small Danish workshops, where machines were used to speed manufacture while hand-fitting and finishing were retained to ensure that quality was not compromised. Leon generally works with one or two assistants. They work under his direct supervision, principally on production runs for designs which originated as individual commissions. Leon makes critical decisions on timber selection and directs the detailing of each piece.

When asked what commissions pleased him most, he nominated writing desks and spoke enthusiastically when describing some features of the twelve he has made over the years. He claims those clients who commissioned writing tables have been particularly stimulating to work with, as the brief reflected both their personal and professional requirements. A clergyman requested a light table to be used as a personal retreat, while a pathologist needed a complex, well-organised space for a microscope, computer hardware, personal files and a clear writing area. Leon acknowledges the importance of these desks in his professional growth as a designer. With each commission it is possible to trace a progressive refinement in the sectional sizes of components and development of detail. Only two writing tables have been made without a personal brief: the table commissioned by the Australian Armed Forces as a wedding gift to Prince Charles and Lady Diana, and a table commissioned by the Powerhouse Museum in Sydney for its furniture collection.

The commission for 93 benches for the New Parliament House in Canberra was undoubtedly the greatest professional challenge in his career. It was a brilliant concept, to involve the maximum number of master craftsmen in the furnishing and decoration of the interior of this national building, providing an opportunity for many Australian woodworkers to undertake work on a scale not previously available. The brief for Leon Sadubin was open, the requirements being that the benches be made from Australian timbers in two lengths with identical width and height. Leon presented a number of concepts to Aldo Giurgola, the project architect, and finally produced a scale model which not only satisfied the brief but solved the logistical problems of manufacturing a large number of long benches in such a small workshop. This commission dominated the production of his workshop for 14 months. When I visited him in 1988, he had almost completed the production run and was looking forward to returning to smaller commissions, grizzling about unloading timber trucks and handling large

**Writing table, scrub beefwood and silky oak.**
Photographer: Scott Donkin.

**Games table, silver ash, blackwood and ebony.**
Photographer: Roger Hanlon.

**Refectory table, blackwood, 1976, 3.6m long.**

sections of Australian hardwood.

Professional growth is a cumulative process in learning. A project of these dimensions provided a valuable lesson in working with architects to tight deadlines and managing a workshop efficiently. He believes, however, that his early refectory tables were equally significant as signposts in his career and are the most free-spirited manifestations of his work. His first refectory tables were made from New Guinea walnut and Tasmanian blackwood, and broke new ground in using whole flitches. Defects in surfaces and edges were shaped and feathered in harmony with grain pattern and colour to emphasise the natural form of each member. Using defects as a design detail is quite common, but to do this effectively requires sensitivity to the material and restrained treatment of those characteristics. Scale is another problem, as to be true to its intent, the table must look massive without being clumsy or gross. Leon's skill is in making this organic table look as strong as a railway bridge trestle but appear light enough to be easily lifted. These refectory tables were significant in launching Leon on his career and ensuring that a number of admiring clients would become patrons.

Decorative details feature increasingly in Leon's work. They are usually of contrasting timbers and are complementary in colour and figure to the ground timber. Quite often the treatment is subtle, and one has to examine the inlay closely to appreciate its contribution to the design. His use of more overt decorations is limited to the ends of writing tables, where there is a need to provide a break in a large surface rather than an embellishment. In his own words: 'Decoration has to be part of the total design, and it's essential that the proportions of each member within a piece are correct. I spend much of my time with sketches and prototypes, getting those proportions right. I want the piece to be light yet not fragile. At the same time, I don't want it to appear earthbound. The final structure must be harmonious, both in detail and in the sum of the parts. I hope that others can recognise restraint and economy in my work, because it's something I'm continually striving for. When exposed jointing can add something significant to a design I consider its use, but not to demonstrate skill. I find it a great challenge to ensure that each piece is a simple statement of design.

'I am fascinated by texture in timber. It's something I'd like to explore further in the future. Although I was born in Israel and arrived in Australia when I was nine years old, I feel very much Australian and I would like to think my work says something about this environment of ours. To express this texture is one means of relating to that environment.'

It is necessary to be pragmatic about design if a woodworker is to remain solvent. Leon equates managing a workshop with walking a tightrope, continually balancing the wish to remain a creative artist with the restrictive demands of a business which must pay its way. Leon keeps a folder of commissions and a separate sketchbook of ideas in which designs are progressively refined and finally translated into two or three innovative pieces each year. He admits that without these pieces he would find it difficult to maintain his enthusiasm. His priorities in business and design have been modified with success and experience. That is not to suggest that he has compromised his professional integrity, but rather that he has grown as a designer.

One of the most difficult activities is marketing creative furniture. Although Leon Sadubin has been successful at both promoting and selling, he regrets that there is no organisation in Australia similar to *Den Permanente* in Denmark, where a permanent display of outstanding craftwork from throughout the country could be maintained.

Many of his clients see hand-crafted furniture as a worthwhile investment, something to be handed on as family heirlooms after loving use, an encouraging concept in our consumer-led society. The small proportion of the population who can afford to provide this patronage is no doubt growing, as is their knowledge of furniture and designers. Leon Sadubin has done more than most to foster this growth in clients who appreciate the daily use of a finely crafted chair to sit at, or a meal shared with others at an interesting table. I am hopeful that the community at large will grow to appreciate the contribution made by Leon and his fellow designer-makers. Theirs is a contribution to national identity, its expression of lifestyle and, of course, enjoyment.

**Benches for the New Parliament House being assembled in Leon Sadubin's workshop.** Photographer: Leon Sadubin.

**Leon Sadubin's benches in the New Parliament House, Canberra.** Photographer: Anna Brenan.

# Refectory Table

We have come to accept dining tables as refined pieces of furniture, usually rectangular or circular in shape and permanently located in a dining room. This has not always been so, as space in most homes was at a premium and a table was used for whatever purpose was appropriate at a particular time of day. Leon Sadubin's refectory tables were influenced by the old slab tables he saw in Norway and by hand-hewn 'bush' furniture made by the early settlers in Australia.

Leon's refectory table is assembled without glue in a matter of minutes, and is as robust and stable as were the tables of old. It is different not only in its structural refinement, but it appears to be 'of the tree' from which it was made. It is a modern sculptured table, yet timeless in design.

## Making the table

Leon Sadubin's first refectory table was more than three metres long, the length of the blackwood flitches he had selected. Subsequent tables have been scaled down, and are now made in three lengths, from 2.0 to 2.5 metres. The shape of the top is primarily determined by the dressed shape of the flitches. If the shapes, with the sapwood removed, are complementary and of sufficient width, two flitches will suffice. If the flitches are not wide enough after shaping, a centre panel can be used, as in the table described here.

The table should reflect the shape and grain pattern in the flitches. Do not slavishly follow a predetermined shape — remember that to retain its organic form, the shape should flow sympathetically with the grain pattern and any defect be incorporated into the total design. It may be necessary to scale the other components to the table top if it differs markedly in size from Leon's table.

## Making the top

- Select two flitches and mark long flowing curves on the outer edges to remove the wane edge and sapwood (if it is unstable or defective). Place the flitches roughly in their final position and assess the composition of the curves. Cut the curved edges and select a third flitch for the centre panel.

- Dress all flitches to a thickness of 45mm. Lay out the two outer flitches in their correct relative position, overlay the third flitch on the other two and cramp together. Mark a line on both edges of the centre panel to define the shape, and cut along the lines through both centre and outer flitches. Assemble the three panels and check whether all the curved edges match.

- Cut the ends of all flitches to shape and contour the edges and defects in the surface to produce smooth flowing surfaces.

- Cut the 6mm inlays to shape in a contrasting timber and, using these as templates, mark out the positions of the trenches into which they will fit. Cut the trenches to depth, glue the inlay and dress the surfaces flush.

**Refectory table.**
© **Leon Sadubin.**
Photographer: Scott
Donkin.

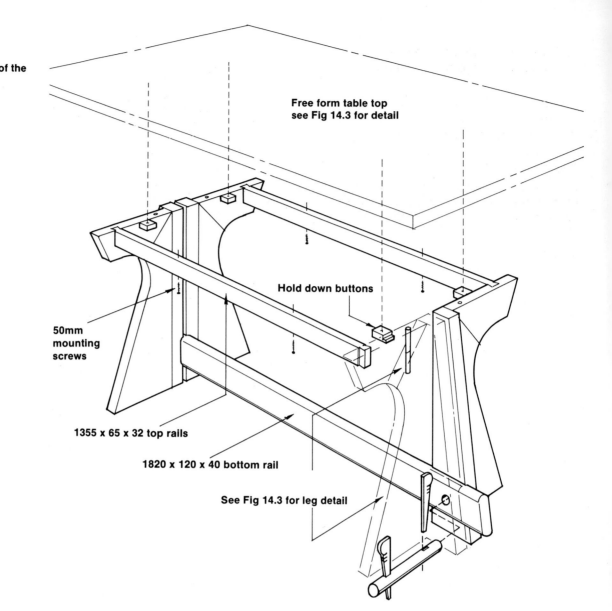

**Fig 14.1 Anatomy of the refectory table.**

Free form table top
see Fig 14.3 for detail

Hold down buttons

50mm mounting screws

1355 x 65 x 32 top rails

1820 x 120 x 40 bottom rail

See Fig 14.3 for leg detail

• The three flitches are aligned with eight brass dowels. Mark the centre of the dowels on corresponding edges and drill holes for the 50mm x 12mm dowels. Note that there will be a 10mm gap between the matching curved edges.

• Assemble the three panels and mark the boundary lines for texturing on the top surface. These lines should not be drawn parallel to the outer edge of each panel, but mark the boundary of a complementary pattern on the surface. Using a 9/15 gouge, make individual cuts in the surface. These cuts should be evenly spaced but not overlapping.

## Making the legs and rails

• The legs are in matched pairs, each made from three separate members which are edge-glued as shown in Fig 14.2.

• Dress the timber for the legs to 55mm thick and mark out the shape of each member as shown in the end view of the table in Fig 14.3. Dress the edges to be glued to give a gap-free joint. Using either biscuits or dowels, align the joints ready for gluing.

• Dress and sand all faces and edges. Glue and assemble the joints and cramp lightly.

• The mitre joints are strengthened with a dowel. Bore an 18mm hole vertically from the top edge of the leg through each joint. Glue and insert the dowel.

• Prepare the two top rails to sectional size 65mm x 32mm and cut to a length of 1365mm. Mark out the dovetail on either end of the rail and leg and cut the joint.

• Counterbore and drill the holes for the four 50mm securing screws used to fix the rails to the table top.

• Prepare the bottom rail to sectional size 120mm x 40mm and cut to a length of 1820mm. Shape the ends and round over the edges with a 20mm round over bit in a router.

• Assemble the table legs in pairs with spacers in place to give a

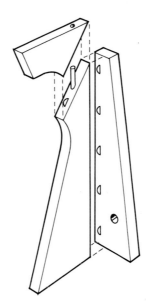

**Fig 14.2 Half leg showing 18mm dowel and use of biscuit joiners.**

**Refectory table**
© **Leon Sadubin.**
Photographer: Scott Donkin.

**Fig 14.3 Construction details for the refectory table.**

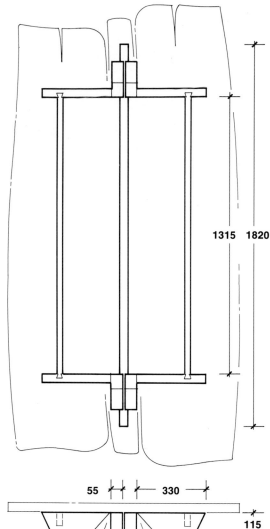

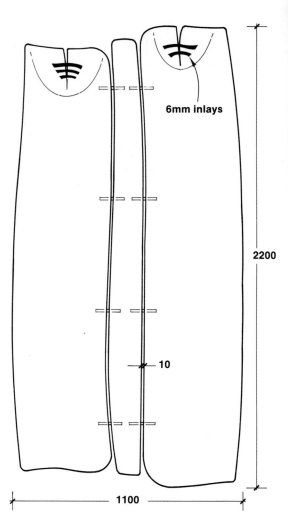

6mm inlays

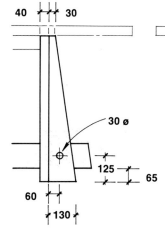

10mm gap. Mark out on each leg the position of the shaped trench into which the bottom rail will fit. Cut the trenches and fit the joint.

● Assemble the rails and legs, and cramp the legs together on the bottom rail. Mark the centre of the two holes for the wedging dowels and bore a 30mm hole for the

dowel through both halves of the leg and the bottom rail.

● Make the 30mm diameter wedging dowel and the wedges.

● Make four screw blocks to fix the legs to the table top, and cut trenches in the legs into which they will fit.

## Assembly and finishing

● Sand all surfaces to a fine finish.

● Apply three coats of buffing oil and sand each coat with 400 grit wet and dry.

● Buff the surfaces.

● Assemble the table.

# Epilogue

In the beginning I promised that, as you read this book, you would come to know more about Australian woodwork and why it was different. Do you now know what it is that makes the work of Australian woodworkers distinctive? Is it unique? I can predict that these questions will often have been asked by those who have taken the trouble to read the profiles and study how the pieces were made. Obviously most of the techniques used have a foreign source, and no doubt my earlier statement, that we are influenced by everything in our global environment, has been substantiated by what is presented here. The ideas are principally Western in origin, as is the function of the furniture. Australians are 'Westerners', with British and European values, but are geographically 'fringe-dwellers', influenced but not bound by those parent cultures.

What *is* undoubtedly different is the timber worked by these woodworkers, the freedom with which they work it and the innovation this promotes. I have been fascinated by what influenced their decisions in designing and making. The question was asked obliquely at the beginning, would their work be different if they had lived and worked in Wandsworth or Wapping? The answer is undoubtedly *yes*. David Tucker may resist the influence of the bush that surrounds him, but it pervades his every hour. What he creates is undoubtedly different to what he would have made in Somerset if he had returned 'home'. For others like Gay Hawkes, Kevin Perkins and Robert Parker, the Australian landscape and its forests *are* their inspiration, the source of their powers of expression and what they return to repeatedly for renewal. I will leave it as said that their work is at one end of a spectrum of influence, and leave it for you to decide on the placement of the other woodworkers on a progressive ladder towards conformity. I will not attempt to expand on what I mean by 'conformity' in an Australian context, nor how that may relate to 'conformity' in the United Kingdom or USA. No doubt when you have read these last words and the book that has preceded them, you will have already developed opinions on this subject. I hope that you will discuss them with others.

# Index

# Metric Conversion

## Inches to Millimetres and Centimetres

**MM** millimetres     **CM** centimetres

| Inches | MM | CM | Inches | CM | Inches | CM |
|--------|-----|------|--------|------|--------|-------|
| ⅛ | 3 | 0.3 | 9 | 22.9 | 30 | 76.2 |
| ¼ | 6 | 0.6 | 10 | 25.4 | 31 | 78.7 |
| ⅜ | 10 | 1.0 | 11 | 27.9 | 32 | 81.3 |
| ½ | 13 | 1.3 | 12 | 30.5 | 33 | 83.8 |
| ⅝ | 16 | 1.6 | 13 | 33.0 | 34 | 86.4 |
| ¾ | 19 | 1.9 | 14 | 35.6 | 35 | 88.9 |
| ⅞ | 22 | 2.2 | 15 | 38.1 | 36 | 91.4 |
| 1 | 25 | 2.5 | 16 | 40.6 | 37 | 94.0 |
| 1¼ | 32 | 3.2 | 17 | 43.2 | 38 | 96.5 |
| 1½ | 38 | 3.8 | 18 | 45.7 | 39 | 99.1 |
| 1¾ | 44 | 4.4 | 19 | 48.3 | 40 | 101.6 |
| 2 | 51 | 5.1 | 20 | 50.8 | 41 | 104.1 |
| 2½ | 64 | 6.4 | 21 | 53.3 | 42 | 100.7 |
| 3 | 76 | 7.6 | 22 | 55.9 | 43 | 109.2 |
| 3½ | 89 | 8.9 | 23 | 58.4 | 44 | 111.8 |
| 4 | 102 | 10.2 | 24 | 61.0 | 45 | 114.3 |
| 4½ | 114 | 11.4 | 25 | 63.5 | 46 | 116.8 |
| 5 | 127 | 12.7 | 26 | 66.0 | 47 | 119.4 |
| 6 | 152 | 15.2 | 27 | 68.6 | 48 | 121.9 |
| 7 | 178 | 17.8 | 28 | 71.1 | 49 | 124.5 |
| 8 | 203 | 20.3 | 29 | 73.7 | 50 | 127.0 |

# Biography

Tom Darby was a teacher of industrial arts in New South Wales for twenty years, specialising in woodwork, technical drawing and engineering science. He was subsequently appointed deputy principal of a Central Coast high school before becoming an Inspector of Schools in industrial arts in 1975, being responsible for curriculum development and teacher in-service. On his retirement in 1987, he changed direction and, with his wife Margaret, opened a business, Baringa Woodcrafts. He now designs and makes custom-built furniture.

He has travelled widely and has visited many craftsmen and galleries, not only in all the Australian states, but also in the USA and Europe. His articles on individual Australian craftspeople have appeared in *Woodworking*, *Woodworking International* and *Woodworkingtoday*.

# WOODWORKING

| | | | |
|---|---|---|---|
| 40 More Woodworking Plans & Projects | GMC Publications | Making Shaker Furniture | Barry Jackson |
| Bird Boxes and Feeders for the Garden | Dave Mackenzie | Pine Furniture Projects for the Home | Dave Mackenzie |
| Complete Woodfinishing | Ian Hosker | Routing for Beginners | Anthony Bailey |
| Electric Woodwork | Jeremy Broun | Sharpening Pocket Reference Book | Jim Kingshott |
| Furniture & Cabinetmaking Projects | GMC Publications | Sharpening: The Complete Guide | Jim Kingshott |
| Furniture Projects | Rod Wales | Space-Saving Furniture Projects | Dave Mackenzie |
| Furniture Restoration (Practical Crafts) | Kevin Jan Bonner | Stickmaking: A Complete Course | Andrew Jones & Clive George |
| Furniture Restoration and Repair for Beginners | Kevin Jan Bonner | Test Reports: The Router and | |
| Green Woodwork | Mike Abbott | Furniture & Cabinetmaking | GMC Publications |
| The Incredible Router | Jeremy Broun | Veneering: A Complete Course | Ian Hosker |
| Making & Modifying Woodworking Tools | Jim Kingshott | Woodfinishing Handbook (Practical Crafts) | Ian Hosker |
| Making Chairs and Tables | GMC Publications | Woodworking Plans and Projects | GMC Publications |
| Making Fine Furniture | Tom Darby | The Workshop | Jim Kingshott |
| Making Little Boxes from Wood | John Bennett | | |

# WOODTURNING

| | | | |
|---|---|---|---|
| Adventures in Woodturning | David Springett | Practical Tips for Woodturners | GMC Publications |
| Bert Marsh: Woodturner | Bert Marsh | Spindle Turning | GMC Publications |
| Bill Jones' Notes from the Turning Shop | Bill Jones | Turning Miniatures in Wood | John Sainsbury |
| Bill Jones' Further Notes from the Turning Shop | Bill Jones | Turning Wooden Toys | Terry Lawrence |
| Colouring Techniques for Woodturners | Jan Sanders | Understanding Woodturning | Ann & Bob Phillips |
| The Craftsman Woodturner | Peter Child | Useful Techniques for Woodturners | GMC Publications |
| Decorative Techniques for Woodturners | Hilary Bowen | Useful Woodturning Projects | GMC Publications |
| Essential Tips for Woodturners | GMC Publications | Woodturning: Bowls, Platters, Hollow Forms, Vases, | |
| Faceplate Turning | GMC Publications | Vessels, Bottles, Flasks, Tankards, Plates | GMC Publications |
| Fun at the Lathe | R.C. Bell | Woodturning: A Foundation Course | Keith Rowley |
| Illustrated Woodturning Techniques | John Hunnex | Woodturning: A Source Book of Shapes | John Hunnex |
| Intermediate Woodturning Projects | GMC Publications | Woodturning Jewellery | Hilary Bowen |
| Keith Rowley's Woodturning Projects | Keith Rowley | Woodturning Masterclass | Tony Boase |
| Make Money from Woodturning | Ann & Bob Phillips | Woodturning Techniques | GMC Publications |
| Multi-Centre Woodturning | Ray Hopper | Woodturning Tools & Equipment Test Reports | GMC Publications |
| Pleasure and Profit from Woodturning | Reg Sherwin | Woodturning Wizardry | David Springett |
| Practical Tips for Turners & Carvers | GMC Publications | | |

# WOODCARVING

| | | | |
|---|---|---|---|
| The Art of the Woodcarver | GMC Publications | Understanding Woodcarving | GMC Publications |
| Carving Birds & Beasts | GMC Publications | Understanding Woodcarving in the Round | GMC Publications |
| Carving on Turning | Chris Pye | Useful Techniques for Woodcarvers | GMC Publications |
| Carving Realistic Birds | David Tippey | Wildfowl Carving – Volume 1 | Jim Pearce |
| Decorative Woodcarving | Jeremy Williams | Wildfowl Carving – Volume 2 | Jim Pearce |
| Essential Tips for Woodcarvers | GMC Publications | The Woodcarvers | GMC Publications |
| Essential Woodcarving Techniques | Dick Onians | Woodcarving: A Complete Course | Ron Butterfield |
| Lettercarving in Wood: A Practical Course | Chris Pye | Woodcarving: A Foundation Course | Zoë Gertner |
| Power Tools for Woodcarving | David Tippey | Woodcarving for Beginners | GMC Publications |
| Practical Tips for Turners & Carvers | GMC Publications | Woodcarving Tools & Equipment Test Reports | GMC Publications |
| Relief Carving in Wood: A Practical Introduction | Chris Pye | Woodcarving Tools, Materials & Equipment | Chris Pye |

# UPHOLSTERY

| | | | |
|---|---|---|---|
| Seat Weaving (Practical Crafts) | Ricky Holdstock | Upholstery Restoration | David James |
| Upholsterer's Pocket Reference Book | David James | Upholstery Techniques & Projects | David James |
| Upholstery: A Complete Course | David James | | |

# TOYMAKING

| | | | |
|---|---|---|---|
| Designing & Making Wooden Toys | Terry Kelly | Restoring Rocking Horses | Clive Green & Anthony Dew |
| Fun to Make Wooden Toys & Games | Jeff & Jennie Loader | Scrollsaw Toy Projects | Ivor Carlyle |
| Making Board, Peg & Dice Games | Jeff & Jennie Loader | Wooden Toy Projects | GMC Publications |
| Making Wooden Toys & Games | Jeff & Jennie Loader | | |